D1131978

ENAMELING

ENAMELING
A Step-by-Step Guide

BY
MAURINE
REMINIH

ILLUSTRATIONS BY
ANN BRUCE
CHAMBERLAIN

GALAHAD BOOKS · NEW YORK

Library of Congress Catalog Card Number: 73-90224
ISBN 0-88365-170-X
Published by arrangement with Nash Publishing Corporation

Manufactured in the United States of America

CONTENTS

ENAMELING

CHAPTER 1
GETTING TO KNOW YOUR MEDIUM

Enameling on metal is one of the most exciting, most rewarding, and most challenging arts any craftsman could ask for. As a medium for using color to express mood, it is unsurpassed.

With enameling, the artisan can create objects of great beauty even though he has had none of the formal training in drawing and painting so necessary to the artist in oils or watercolors. The work he turns out in enameling can have all the impact of modern graphics, but with only a fraction of the labor those graphics involve. He may even play about with sculptural techniques, if it so pleases him.

But the basic attraction of enameling, possibly, is in the appeal it makes to some primitive instinct in the craftsman. Working with raw copper and raw glass (well—almost raw!), the artist employs that basic element, fire, to do his bidding.

The copper and the glass are fused, and it is he, the artist, who has masterminded the whole thing. There is a fascination about the alchemy of metal, glass, and fire that is inescapable.

Behind all the excitement of the creation of enameled pieces, and the elation of their successful completion, there is a great deal of painstaking, patient preparation. Slapdash work never comes off in enameling. What may appear to be a casual, spontaneous composition has much carefully planned work behind it.

In the pages to follow, we will endeavor to lead the beginner through the various stages of enameling, from the simple application of a single coat of color to a copper piece, on through all the other stages to the more intricate techniques of cloisonné and champlevé. We will keep the directions as simple and as basic as we can, not because we underestimate the intelligence of the reader, but because there is no necessity for cluttering instructions with irrelevant asides and confusing elaborations.

We assume that the reader, having shown an interest in enameling, is endowed with an imagination that will push him on toward exploring all the avenues available to him. We desire only to provide him with the keys which will open the doors to those avenues.

BASIC MUSTS

In all enameling, there are several basics to be observed, no matter if the artist is creating a simple one-color enamel piece, or an intricate cloisonné design.

Basic number one is simply this: *the metal must be clean.*

By clean we do not mean simply free of dirt and smudges, visually clean; it must be chemically clean, with all grease removed from its surface.

There are several ways to attain this cleanliness.

The time-tried method is with the acid bath. The copper piece is submerged in a solution of one part nitric acid to four parts water, and allowed to remain there until it reaches a fresh pink color. In preparing the acid solution, remember to use a glass tray, and always *pour acid into water* never water into acid. Handle the copper piece with wooden or copper tongs, and take great care not to splash the solution onto skin or clothing. The room in which you are working should be well ventilated—fumes from the acid can be toxic. Once the project is completed, the acid solution may be discarded by pouring it down the drain, *if* this is done carefully and the cold water tap is allowed to run fully at the same time. Continue the cold water flushing for some minutes, to make sure all the solution has passed through the plumbing pipes.

If you are working with small children, in elementary-school groups or Scout-handicraft groups, you may not want to be involved with anything as potentially dangerous as the nitric acid solution. You may use a substitute cleaning solution which is completely harmless—vinegar and salt. Use 1½ tablespoons of salt to each cup of vinegar. It may take a bit longer to clean the copper with this solution, but it does have the advantage of presenting no menace to young hobbyists.

There are also several commercial copper cleaners available at craft and hobby supply stores. These will do the job too. But they are much more expensive to use than either the nitric acid or the vinegar-and-salt solutions.

Following this cleaning bath, the copper piece should be

swabbed with a clean cloth soaked in nonsoapy detergent, then rinsed thoroughly under running water.

If the water does not bead up on the surface of the copper, if it runs off in even sheets, then the copper is sufficiently clean to proceed with the enameling.

This cleaning process is to be followed whether you are attempting the beginning project described in Chapter Three, or are starting off on your three-thousandth enameling project. It must always be followed. It should become a routine operation with the enamelist.

Testing

Another procedure which should become automatic with enamelists is color testing. Before you begin even the simplest of projects, find out what your colors will do in the kiln.

To run these tests, cut a square of 18-gauge copper into small rectangles—about the size of two ordinary postage stamps will do nicely—coat the small rectangle with adhesive, then sift on a layer of powdered enamel. Give it several minutes to dry, then place it in the preheated kiln. Fire one test sample for two minutes. Prepare a second rectangle just as you did the first, but fire it for three minutes. Do this for each color you plan to use on any piece, and as soon as each test sample has cooled, scratch on the reverse side notes indicating both time and temperature. A 1500–2 would mean you had fired it at 1500 degrees for two minutes, for instance.

By running tests in this manner on each color you plan to use in any project, you can avoid many of the mistakes you might make without testing. You will discover for yourself just what colors burn out fast, and what colors take the longest to fuse.

And a little practical suggestion here. Don't throw those test pieces away once you're finished with them. Collect them in one container after each project is completed. Someday you'll have enough of them to be used, mosaic-fashion, in a patchwork enamel table top for the patio, or to line a big serving tray.

Know Your Colors

Each of the colors in your palette has its own peculiar properties. There are soft-fusing enamels—those which melt at low temperatures. And there are hard-fusing enamels—those which take a higher temperature to melt.

Most enameling supply catalogs list whether the powdered enamels they offer are soft-, medium-, or hard-fusing. Most hobby shops stock the medium-fusing type. Ask the craft dealer if you are unsure.

But even within these three categories different colors react in different ways. It won't take you long to discover this for yourself. To give you a head start, we list below a few of the things you should anticipate.

Blacks—a dense black enamel should be washed carefully, since it is easily clouded by dust and powder. Blacks tend to burn out easily, and are not acid-resistant, unless you are careful to stipulate that you want a hard-fusing black. A well-stocked palette should contain all three grades of blacks.

Whites—almost the same conditions apply for whites as for blacks, with the softer-fusing whites burning out easily, and being affected by acids. There are, however, a number of gradations of whites, from soft to hard.

Grays—these seem to have a tendency to pit. This is no real problem, since they can be patched easily. Although gray seems a drab, uninteresting color, don't ignore it in assembling your palette, since it is often most effective when used as a foil to the brighter, more advancing colors.

Flux—this is the colorless enamel, often used as a base coat when the raw copper is to show through on the finished piece. There are three grades of flux; the grade you use will be determined by the grade of color you plan to use with it.

Blue—this is the classic choice for background color, and darker shades are often used as counterenamel. Blues are permanent, and not affected by acid. Cobalt seems to be the shade most people think of when they speak of enamels. Remember that transparent blues wash out when applied over raw copper. Use the transparent blues on silver, over foil, or over a base coat of opaque white.

Green—practically the same rules apply to greens as to blues. Transparents are lost over raw copper; opaques are permanent and acid-resistant. Greens are unpredictable, though. Different shades of green react differently to the same temperature, so run those tests first.

Brown—a good, reliable color, as one might guess. The transparents are particularly effective used over raw copper, with the warm tones of the metal shining through. The opaque beige is a very hard color, resistant to wear and acid.

Red—This color has well earned its reputation as a color signifying danger. Reds can spell trouble in the kiln. They are especially soft, burning out more easily than any other color. At high temperatures they may simply disappear. Many enamelists get the best results when reds are fired over a base coat of opaque white. Remember to wash reds well, since the slightest contamination will render them cloudy. Remember, too, to watch for a black edge forming around patches of red when it is fired next to another color. It is possible to plan for this and to integrate it into your design. But, unless you make it work for you, it can be a headache. In any event, technically and aesthetically, reds should be used with restraint in any design.

Washing and Storing Enamels

Still another routine operation, for the beginner or for the advanced enamelist, is the preparation of the enamels to be used for each project. The absolute beginner may not care too much about clear versus cloudy colors, and may be concerned only with getting on with the project. But as skill advances, and more perfection is sought in each project, it should become routine to wash the powdered enamels.

To do this, the enamel is poured into a small jar—one sufficiently large to hold the enamel and about twice its bulk in distilled water. (Don't use tap water—it contains minerals and impurities that will show up in the kiln!) The enamel is agitated, either by stirring with a glass or plastic rod, or by shaking, until the water becomes cloudy. That cloudy water is poured off, more distilled water added to the enamel, and the process repeated. This is done to the point where the pour-off water is no longer cloudy; thus you have flushed the enamel free of all dust and foreign matter that might cause it to become cloudy in the firing.

When the pour-off water is finally clear, spread the washed enamel on a clean paper and allow it to dry. When dry, the clean enamel may be stored in clean screw-top jars. Baby-food jars are ideal for this purpose. Careful storage will eliminate the necessity of frequent washings of the enamel. Even so, a long-stored container of enamel should be washed, just in case temperature and humidity fluctuations have caused some disintegration within the enamel.

Why All This Trouble?

It is only when the copper has been painstakingly cleaned, and the enamels washed clear of impurities, that all the effort you put into creating a beautiful piece of enamel will pay off. The most beautiful design is wasted if the enamel doesn't adhere to the copper, or if the surface of the enamel has a cloudy, milky look. Just remind yourself that the piece you are creating may last two thousand years! Then the few extra minutes you spend doing the job right will seem no time at all.

CHAPTER 2
WHAT
YOU WILL NEED

Copper enameling can be a hobby for almost any budget.

If you have unlimited funds, there are ever so many gadgets and gismos and bits of equipment you may acquire. But the beauty of the hobby is that none of these more expensive pieces is really necessary. Enameling can be done with a minimum outlay of cash for equipment.

On the assumption that you will find your own way to spend extra money for extra accessories, we will list the absolute basics for the craft. And, because we realize that, to be a beginner, a "sifter" could mean a flour sifter, and a "Nichrome-mesh trivet" could mean nothing at all, we will describe each piece of equipment and briefly explain its use. Knowing what it is, and how it is used, will be a big step toward using it correctly.

Reduced to basics, copper enameling calls for:

1. A kiln
2. Copper, either in precut shapes, or sheet stock

3. Powdered enamels in as many colors as you want and/or can afford; also clear flux
4. Lumps and threads of enamel
5. Sifter
6. Atomizer or sprayer
7. Brushes
8. Tweezers
9. Tongs
10. Spatula
11. Adhesive—either gum tragacanth or agar solution
12. Stilts
13. Nichrome-mesh rack
14. Spreader, wet inlay tools, etc.
15. Pyrex tray for acid bath
16. Nitric acid (or alternative solution for cleaning, see Chapter One)
17. Asbestos pad
18. File
19. Emery cloth
20. Carborundum stone

All of the aforementioned supplies are relatively inexpensive, with the exception of the kiln. Some may even be substituted for by using homemade equipment. More on that as we go along.

KILNS

A kiln can be purchased for approximately ten dollars—or you can spend several hundred dollars for it. Table-top kilns, ranging from the smallest with dimensions of three-inch diameter, to a kiln with a seven-inch diameter, are available at most hobby shops. These often come in kits and include complete basic supplies, with a price range up to about thirty dollars.

There are purists among enamelists who look condescendingly on these small kilns. But they are generally the professionals, the almost-pros, or the would-be-pros—all with short memories. They have forgotten what it is like to begin the craft, unsure and untutored. Remember, also, that there are Rolls-Royce owners who look down their noses at owners of Fords.

The table-top kiln will do a job, and do it well. Especially for beginners who are not yet sure how deeply they want to get involved in enameling, the table-top kiln is a perfect solution. And many an artist who graduated to a larger, more professional-type kiln has kept his small table-top kiln in use.

If you decide, after having experimented with the projects outlined in this book, that you are really hooked on enameling and want to go on to bigger and better things, you will probably be looking for a thermostatically controlled kiln.

These kilns are larger, quite a bit more expensive, take up more room and use more electricity. But they have one tremendous advantage; you can control the temperature just as you can control your oven temperature. This means that you can keep very accurate time/temperature records for specific colors and *know* how to duplicate that gorgeous shade of blue you accidentally discovered.

The directions that come with these kilns will give you specific instructions for operation of the model you have purchased.

TABLE TOP

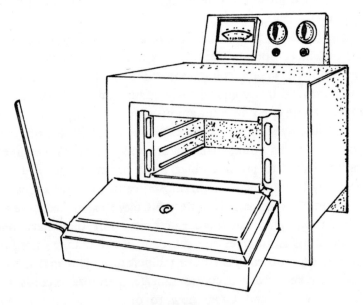

THERMOSTATICALLY
CONTROLLED

Fig. 1
Kilns

Occasionally, bargains can be found in used kilns. Study the catalogs of suppliers (a list of these is in the back of this book) so that you are familiar with the kilns available, and their prices. Otherwise, you won't know a bargain if you stumble across one. And be advised that replacement heating units for kilns are relatively inexpensive. If the used kiln you find is enough of a bargain, you can afford to replace the element, if that becomes necessary. Just be sure the used kiln is solid and has no cracks, and that the door fits snugly for heat-sealing, and opens smoothly and easily.

If you are unsure of just how to use the kiln, you can always write to the manufacturer for a set of instructions, being sure to supply him with the model and serial number so he knows exactly which instructions to send.

And a word of caution! Do not, in ignorance, buy a used or a new kiln designed solely for firing ceramics. These are top loading and, for enameling, present entirely too many problems. When working with ceramics, the piece is put into a cold kiln, fired, allowed to cool in the kiln, and then removed from a cold kiln.

In enameling, the work is put into the kiln after the temperature has reached maximum, and is taken out within minutes. It is almost impossible to do this safely and comfortably with a top-loading kiln.

The thermostatically controlled kiln you buy could have a door that folds down to form a shelf. Or the door could be hinged to swing right or left, or even lift up. Most home enamelists seem to prefer the side-hinged doors, since they allow the door to be opened a crack for visual checking without much heat loss. Ideally, a kiln would have a tiny peep-hole window. But not a top loader—remember!

COPPER

Beginners will probably be happy to settle for the stock shapes readily available at any craft shop carrying copper enameling supplies. These can be found in squares and circles, ovals and oblongs, flower, bird, fish, butterfly, poodle shapes—name it, and they've probably cut copper in that shape. Or the eighteen-gauge copper can be bought in various sized sheets, so that the ambitious or advanced craftsman may fashion his own shapes. Somewhat more difficult to find, but obtainable, is sheet copper in sixteen gauge—suitable for larger pieces such as trays, and for shaping.

ENAMELS

Most beginners will be content with the small vials of enamel colors available at the craft shops or from craft catalogs. Many of these come with sifter tops. (Just be sure to remove the cardboard disc from inside the shaker top, or you won't get much action.) As you grow more experienced, you will want to buy your enamels in larger quantities, which is really more economical in the long run.

In every beginning assortment of enamels there should also be at least one clear flux. If you are limited to buying only one type, get the medium fusing. Ideally, you would also keep both the soft-and-hard fusing clear flux.

Later, you may even want to make a try at grinding your own enamels. For this you buy the bulk frit—enamel in lump form—and a mortar and pestle. Purists insist that the mortar and pestle be of agate—but that is unmercifully expensive. Not-so-purists will find they can do a most adequate job with either porcelain or glass mortar and pestle. It's a time-consuming, exacting job—grinding and sifting, grinding and sifting—but the satisfaction that comes from a purely do-it-yourself job is sufficient compensation for many.

LUMPS AND THREADS

Most kits for beginners come with a small assortment of glass lumps, and another small assortment of glass threads. If you are not working from such a kit, you will find these assortments available at your craft shop, in small containers priced at under one dollar each. You can buy them in assorted colors, or in a single color. For the beginner, the assortment is probably preferable. Until you've experimented with them (see Chapter Seven) you'll have no way of knowing your color preference, or whether you prefer lumps over threads, or vice versa. But they are really indispensable, used by themselves for spots and streaks of color, or as the medium for scrolling and swirling.

SIFTER

If your vials of powdered enamel do not have sifter tops, you will have to buy a sifter. Even if they do come equipped with those sifter tops, it's a good idea to get the feel of using a separate sifter. These little gadgets, resembling a Lilliputian tea strainer, can be had in diameters of one-half inch, one inch, and three inches. If you can get all three sizes, fine and dandy. They should cost you less than three dollars for the set. But if you must keep it to one sifter, buy the smallest size. With it, covering a large area may take a little longer. But with the larger size, covering a small area is an impossibility. Sifters are available in much more expensive models, if you're more comfortable working with expensive equipment. You can also buy the eighty-square mesh screening and make your own, but the saving effected seems hardly worth the effort.

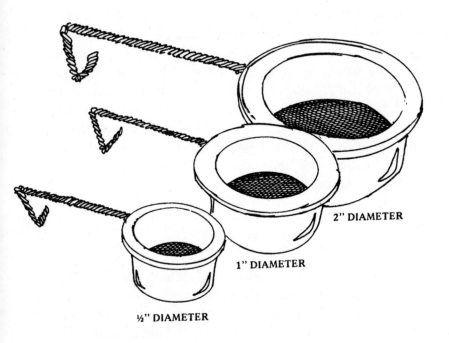

2" DIAMETER

1" DIAMETER

½" DIAMETER

Fig. 2
Sifters

BRUSHES

You will need several small brushes, for painting the surface of the copper piece with adhesive before sifting on the base coat, for applying a design in adhesive, for using with wet enamel projects. Here again purists hold out for expensive sable brushes. But less expensive brushes will do the job, and do it well. Just be careful that whatever brush you're using is tightly bound and not shedding hairs all over your design. These hairs can be fiendishly difficult to pluck out of the enamel, but unless you get every last one of them, they'll burn out and destroy your design.

TWEEZERS

You'll find these little darlings come in handy for a myriad of jobs, such as, removing foreign particles that have strayed

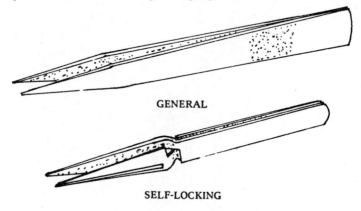

GENERAL

SELF-LOCKING

Fig. 3
Tweezers

onto your enamel piece, as we've mentioned above; arranging and rearranging the lumps and threads into a pleasing design; dipping a just-fired piece into the acid cleaning bath, and remove it therefrom. They are a must-have. And they need not all be the expensive craft-shop variety. Often tweezers about to be discarded from your own medicine chest will still be usable for craft-shop work.

SPRAYER

Although adhesives may be put on the cleaned copper with a brush, before the enamel is sifted into place, many enamelists feel they can obtain a more even coat of adhesive by using a sprayer. This need not be an expensive model. The throat spray atomizer you pick up at the pharmacy will do the job, and can be found for under two dollars.

Fig. 4
Sprayer

ADHESIVE

In any gathering of three or more enamelists, you can probably work up a lively discussion, if not an actual argument, about the relative merits of gum tragacanth over agar as an adhesive in copper enameling—or vice versa. It is a moot question. Only experimentation with each will help you to arrive at your own favorite. Both gum tragacanth and agar are available in ready-to-use solution form. But they are much more expensive that way. In time, you will probably want to prepare your own, if only for economy reasons. Two teaspoons of powdered gum tragacanth in a pint of distilled water (prepared according to directions on the gum-tragacanth package) will give you a pint of adhesive solution for approximately ten cents. Agar solution will cost about the same amount. A pint of prepared, brand-name adhesive could cost you two dollars or more, depending on where you buy it.

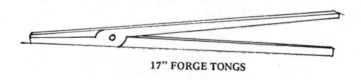

17" FORGE TONGS

SPRING TONGS

Fig. 5
Tongs

TONGS

Another absolute necessity in any enameler's equipment is a pair of tongs. They're really just long-handled, overgrown tweezers. These you will use to grasp the red-hot copper and remove it from the kiln during the annealing process, for handling the piece in its acid bath, and for a number of other duties which you'll think of as you go along. Wooden tongs are best for working with the acid.

SPATULA

A long spatula is another must-have. Once the enamel has been sifted onto a copper piece, the spatula is used to slide under the piece, gently lifting it onto the trivet. The trivet is then placed on the Nichrome-mesh rack—and the spatula used to slide the whole assembly into the kiln. Spatulas can be long and narrow, or shaped like a wedge of pie. So long as they are strong, and have a wooden handle, shape really doesn't make much difference.

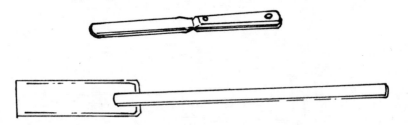

Fig. 6
Spatula

NICHROME WIRE-MESH RACK

Don't make the typical beginner's goof, shrugging off Nichrome wire, and fashioning your own wire-screen rack of some nice, sturdy wire you just happened to have around the house. Most metals, though they won't melt at 1500 degrees, will produce a fire scale that will fly off in all directions, generally peppering your enamel piece with little black specks. Thus the Nichrome, or stainless steel, which does not form fire scale. These racks can be bought ready-made, in sizes from two-inches square, on up.

Fig. 7
Nichrome rack

STILTS

These tiny little objects have an importance to the enameler out of all relation to their size. They keep the copper piece elevated in the kiln, so that the counterenamel does not adhere to the wire rack or the kiln shelf. Made of ceramic, with steel points, the stilts support the piece being fired, so that only three or four tiny points of contact are affected. Avoid the all-ceramic stilts—they were not designed for enameling work.

Here, again, you may find suitable substitutes in unlikely places. For very small pieces, you may find that the small stainless-steel gliders, of the type used on furniture legs, give your copper piece just the right support.

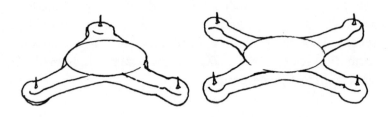

Fig. 8
Stilts

STAINLESS-STEEL TRIVETS

Many counterenameled pieces can be supported for their second and subsequent firings by their very edges—if the piece is placed on the proper size stainless-steel trivet. These are available ready-made in a dizzying variety of shapes and sizes. The simplest seems to be only a rectangle of steel with the four corners turned up at right angles. It should serve most needs, and would even be easy to duplicate in the home workshop—if you have a piece of stainless steel.

Also available now is a sort of do-it-yourself trivet setup, which could be adaptable to many needs. Small refractory blocks may be purchased for less than fifty cents. Nichrome

wire, available at about thirty cents a foot, is cut into short
lengths and pushed into the refractory block at angles, creating a "tailor-made" fit to cradle whatever copper piece you're
working on—large or small.

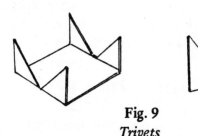

Fig. 9
Trivets

ACID BATH TRAY

For the acid bath to clean your copper shapes before and
between firings, or for the etching process, you will need a
glass tray. The heavy, ovenware-type-glass baking dish would
be quite satisfactory. It should be large enough to accommodate the copper piece easily, and deep enough so that no
acid is splashed over the sides when the copper piece is
lowered into, or removed from, the acid bath. This tray
should always be set on a thick pad of newspapers to protect
the surrounding area.

ASBESTOS PAD

This is a protection for any surface on which you are
working. When the trivet and its red-hot burden are removed
from the kiln, they could make an ugly scar on most any

type of table top. But with an asbestos pad, such damage is avoided. You could buy an asbestos pad from the hobby shop, but you'll probably save money by getting it at the hardware store. And, after all—asbestos is asbestos, no matter what shop it comes from!

Some hobbyists pick up damaged marble slabs at junk yards. These are ideal work surfaces for the enamelist. A ceramic tile counter top is great, too, if you have it.

NITRIC ACID

Bought at hobby shops or hardware stores, nitric acid is to be treated with great respect. Label your bottle with a skull and crossbones and keep well out of reach of children. You will need it for cleaning the copper pieces before the enamel can be applied to them, unless you use one of the alternative methods described in Chapter One. And nitric acid will be necessary if you do any etching, such as in the champlevé technique. Just be sure to remember—*acid goes into water,* never vice versa. Acid solutions no longer needed may be poured down the drain, if you run the cold-water tap full force, both as you carefully pour the acid solution into the drain and for some minutes afterward. It will do no damage to the clay pipe underground, but could harm the iron pipe of the household plumbing unless flushed through very quickly with great quantities of cold water.

FILE

After an enameled piece is finished, it will be necessary to remove fire scale that has built up around the edges, and to smooth the small irregularities along the edges of the enamel itself. A fine jewelry file, preferably of the rat-tail variety, is a necessity in any enamelist's equipment. Remember to file down and away from the center of a piece, never inwardly.

EMERY CLOTH

Even after filing the edges of a finished copper piece, you may find the edges still a little rough to the touch. This is where the emery cloth, which can be purchased in hardware or hobby shops, comes in handy. Carefully rubbing those edges with the cloth, you can smooth the copper and bring it to a fine luster.

CARBORUNDUM STONE

Although a carborundum stone is not an absolute necessity for the beginner on the first few projects, it should be added to your equipment as soon as you graduate to champlevé and cloisonné. Enamel, mounding up within the cloisons, can be smoothed with the carborundum stone as described in the chapters on those techniques. It also comes in handy when it becomes necessary to remove imperfections that have occurred in the firing—the pockmarks left on the enamel's surface by tiny bursting bubbles, for instance.

SPREADERS, SCRIBERS, SCROLLING TOOLS

As in any handcraft work, there are certain jobs that require specific tools. In enameling, the list could go on and on. Swirling tools, for instance, are necessary for that technique. With one swirling tool, the copper is held steady in the kiln, or moved as desired, while the other swirling tool is used to mix the melted enamels. These swirling tools may be inexpensive (less than one dollar each) or you may want to buy the heavier models. Spreaders and scribers are necessary, too—but they could be fashioned at home out of nutpicks or other kitchen equipment. Study the pages of the craft catalogs you'll send for—you'll soon know what you can or cannot live without.

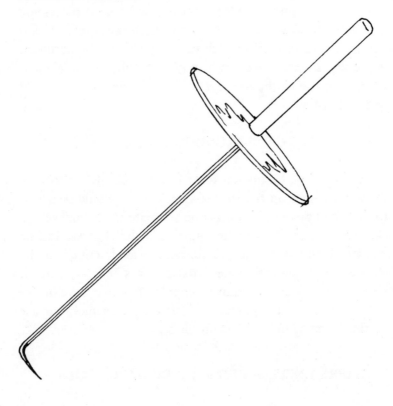

Fig. 10
Swirling tool

CHAPTER 3
START OFF WITH AN EASY ONE

YOU WILL NEED

1 stock copper shape—the type used for pendants (pre-
    punched) either in the shape of a circle, oval or freeform
80-mesh enamel in desired color
Adhesive (gum tragacanth or agar solution)
Brush or atomizer
Sifter
Tongs
Nichrome-wire rack
Trivet
Spatula
Key-chain finding

This first, most elementary project is designed specifically to acquaint you with just how easy it is to turn out something both useful and decorative.

If you followed the suggestion in Chapter One, making test strips of the various colors in your collection of enamels, you already know something of their performance in the kiln. But with those test strips, you had no real need for careful, even distribution of the enamel over the copper, no real reason for paying attention to building up the enamels around the edge of your piece to avoid firing out. Now that you are making something you will be using, you must practice that caution.

We would suggest using a large disc for your copper shape this time. It is available with a hole prepunched close to the edge. And we would suggest enameling it in bright red.

There are several reasons for these choices. For one, a large red disc is easy to find when your keys plummet to the bottom of your purse. For another, red is one of the trickiest colors to fire correctly. You might as well learn, right off, how it should be done.

Before you begin work preparing the piece—plug in your kiln. The manual that came with it should tell you exactly how long the kiln will take to heat up to the desired temperature, but most of the small kilns without thermostats take about forty-five minutes to reach the maximum temperature.

Clean the copper in the nitric acid solution, as described in Chapter One, or with one of the alternative methods listed there. Only when the copper is an even pink color is it ready for removing from the acid bath.

Even after its acid bath, the copper may have some grease adhering to its surface. This may be removed with a clean cloth that has been dipped in a soapless detergent solution. Go over both surfaces well.

The next step is to rinse the piece thoroughly under

running water. This is the time to test the surfaces and see if they are quite clean. If the water flows off the surfaces evenly—does not bead up—then you know all the grease and oil have been removed. Dry the piece thoroughly with a lint-free cloth or tissue, being careful from now on not to touch either top or bottom surface with your hands.

If you inspect the piece closely, you will note that one side is just barely convex in shape, the other concave. Even in so-called flat shapes, there is this domed effect. The top side of the dome, or convex, will be the face side of your piece.

Place the copper, face side *down,* on a piece of clean paper (typing paper works fine—but *not* newspaper). It helps to place the copper piece on top of a penny. Elevating the piece in this way enables you to slide it onto the spatula more easily when you are ready to transfer it to the rack. You are going to *counterenamel* the piece first—that is, enamel the back side to keep it from warping during later firings.

Coat the exposed side with the adhesive solution—a thin, even layer. If you put the adhesive on too thickly, it will run and puddle the enamels. Too thinly, and you'll wind up with bald patches on the copper. The adhesive may be applied with a brush, or sprayed on using an ordinary throat-spray-type atomizer.

When the surface is evenly covered with the adhesive, sift on the enamel. If your small containers of enamel came with sifter tops, you may use them that way. Or you may prefer to transfer the enamel, in small amounts, to the tiny sifter you've bought for that purpose. Sift the enamel evenly, except for the edges of the piece, where there should be a somewhat heavier deposit. Enamel burns away most rapidly around the edges of a copper piece, and should therefore be laid on more heavily at those edges.

When you feel the piece has been properly covered with

the enamel, allow to dry. Drying may be hastened by placing the piece on top of the kiln—but use extreme care that you do not dislodge any of the enamel.

When it is dry, slide it off the penny onto the spatula and from there onto the rack. Lift the rack into the kiln.

Until you've done a few projects, and begin to get the feel of the time it will take in the kiln, you'd probably better keep an eye on the whole process. Leaving the kiln door open a bit will make the firing take a little longer, but you will learn just what happens.

First, the enamel will take on a granular, pebbly surface. Then, slowly, as it liquifies, it will begin to smooth out. For this first firing, which will be the reverse side of your copper piece, remove it from the kiln the moment the surface begins to resemble that of an orange peel. This is the underfired state. Since you will be giving the piece another firing to fuse the top side, it is better to underfire this first coat.

After the piece has been removed, and when it cools, you may discover small imperfections here and there. A bubble formed and burst, perhaps, leaving a tiny pocklike pit in the surface. Or the enamel, spread too sparingly at one point, burned out and left a bald patch. Simply cover these over with more enamel, return to the kiln, and fire again.

Now that the counterenamel job is complete, you may proceed with the face of the piece. Clean off the fire scale which has formed by plunging the piece in the acid bath briefly. Always use copper or wooden tongs when handling the copper shape in the acid. Should you use tongs of some other metal, some of the particles might transfer to your copper piece.

The top surface, cleaned of fire scale, is enameled in precisely the same manner you used for the counterenamel.

Thin but even coat of adhesive, thin coat of enamel, drying, and then firing.

This time, however, the copper is not placed directly on the Nichrome-mesh rack. If you were to do that, the counter-enamel would melt onto the mesh, ruining both the counter-enamel and the rack. Instead, use a trivet. You may use the type where the copper piece is supported by its edges or the type with Nichrome-wire points, which will leave only tiny pinprick marks after the firing.

The copper piece, atop the trivet, is placed on the Nichrome-mesh rack and the entire assembly is lifted into the kiln. This time, allow the firing to go past the dull, orange-peel stage. There comes the magic moment when it turns shiny and glossy and glassy—and you know it has melted and fused to the copper.

It is an exciting moment—whether it's the first piece you've ever done, or the four-thousandth! But don't lose your cool and stand there admiring it while it burns out! Carefully remove copper-trivet-rack from the kiln, as one unit, and place them on the asbestos pad to cool. There is more magic to be witnessed now. As the enameled copper slowly cools, it will change color gradually—until it finally reaches the hue it will be forevermore.

Once the enameled piece has cooled—a process that may take ten minutes or more—there remains only the clean-up job. Any fire scale that has built up around the edges should be removed with a fine file and then emery cloth. Remember to file in long steady strokes, away from the center of the piece. If you file toward the center, you are bound to chip off some of that beautiful enamel you've just labored so hard to apply evenly.

With this initial piece, the clean-up operation is minimal.

Once the copper edge is clean and shining, you may slip the key-chain finding through its little slot—and your very first enamel project has been completed!

CHAPTER 4
TRY A SECOND COLOR

YOU WILL NEED

1 stock copper shape—suitable for a pendant, with hole
    already punched
80-mesh enamels in desired colors
Adhesive (agar or gum tragacanth)
Brush or atomizer
Tongs
Trivet
Nichrome-mesh rack
Jewelry neck-chain, cord, ribbon, or leather thong

The procedure for this second project is identical to that
of the first project—and then one step beyond.

Refer to the directions in the preceding chapter. But begin, now, to memorize the procedure: 1) thorough cleaning; 2) counterenameling; 3) second cleaning to remove fire scale; and 4) enameling base coat on face of copper piece. The only variation from the earlier procedure is to underfire the first coat of enamel on the face of the piece, since you will be giving it additional firings.

When all the above has been done, and the piece is cool, you are ready to go to work with the second color.

Perhaps you have chosen an opaque yellow for the base coat. Why not experiment with a transparent green for your second color. The combinations possible are almost endless—light on dark, dark on light, complementary colors, constrasting colors. Only your own whim will dictate.

Once you've made up your mind what color goes on what, and your copper piece is out of the kiln and cooled, put it on a clean sheet of paper. Cover a portion of the face with a clean scrap of paper—with either a sharp cut edge, or one which has been torn. Lay the "stencil" paper piece diagonally across the face of the enameled copper piece, or straight across—whatever looks best to you. Or cut a curved mask out of paper and use that to block off part of the enameled piece. Whatever suits your fancy.

Paint the exposed portion of the enamel with an even coat of adhesive. Then sift the second color of enamel onto the exposed portion of the piece. Let it pile up most heavily along the edge of the paper, and shade off toward the edges of the piece. Lay your second color on solidly at one point, but not in a heap or pile. Then feather it out subtly, so that much of the base coat shows through.

If you goof at any point along about here—no problem!

Lift the shape with the spatula, spill all the loose enamel onto a clean piece of paper. You may even remove the enamel adhering to the piece with a tissue—just don't touch it with your hands. Put it onto another clean piece of paper, and start all over again.

When you finally have the second color arranged on top the base coat to your satisfaction, lift the stencil paper carefully onto another clean sheet of paper so that the enamel adhering to it may be reclaimed later. If there are any particles of enamel adhering to the portion that was previously fired, remove them with a dampened brush.

After the piece has had a chance to dry completely, place the copper piece on the trivet, both onto the wire rack, and the works into the oven. This time leave it in until the surface has taken on a glassy shine.

You may just get carried away and want to add a third color. Opaque and transparent green on the yellow, perhaps. Follow the same procedure for the third color that you used for the second. Unless it's a hurdy-gurdy, carnival effect you're striving for, it will probably be best to keep the piece to three colors. Introducing more, at this point, could result in a piece that resembles nothing more than a color-sample chart.

A note of caution. After you've finished with each color, pour the remaining grains of enamel carefully back into their vials. The sheet on which you've placed the discarded masking paper may be folded, gently and carefully, to form a trough, so that pouring the granules back into the vial is a simple operation. And it is important that all papers, once used, be discarded. Even microscopic bits of color adhering to the paper might mix with another color, if the paper were to be reused. And those microscopic dots of color attain the dimensions of a locomotive headlamp, if they appear unwanted on a fired piece.

If you should ever goof and mix up your colors—and who among us hasn't done that in a moment of absent-mindedness—don't despair and toss the mixed colors into the trash can. Such mixtures are quite serviceable when used as counterenamels. And if you're counterenameling a flat piece such as a tile, which will be cemented to something, who cares what color you've used on the back side?

CHAPTER 5
CREATE A DESIGN

YOU WILL NEED

2 copper shapes (one-inch diameter circles or shapes of
    your choice)
80-mesh enamel in desired colors
Sifter
Brush
Adhesive
Steel wool or emery cloth
Nichrome-mesh rack
Trivet
Spatula
Earring findings
Epoxy glue or solder

This project should acquaint you with the complete sim-plicity of introducing design into your enamel projects. As in all enameled pieces, there should be more time spent on planning and preparation than on the actual execution of the piece. It is the planning, the designing, that shows up in the final work.

In designing earrings, you will want to consider who will be wearing them. What are her favorite colors—with what costumes might she wear them? Choose your color scheme accordingly. As for the design—how might it express her personality? If she's slightly on the kooky side, perhaps a simple doodle of a tic-tac-toe design in the center of each earring would amuse her; perhaps a stylized floral design would be more appropriate. Give your imagination free rein, but do decide what the design is to be before beginning work on your copper pieces. Ad-lib doodling is only for experi-enced, and inspired, craftsmen.

The surfaces of the copper shapes should be roughed slightly with the steel wool or emery cloth, then cleaned thoroughly as described in the preceding chapter.

Once clean and dry, the copper should never be touched with the hands during the remainder of the enameling process. Use tweezers or tongs, or lift with the spatula.

Place the copper shapes on a clean piece of paper, and coat the back sides with adhesive. Any of the adhesives may be applied with a brush or may be sprayed on with an ordinary throat-spray atomizer. Just be sure to get an even coat—not too thin, and not so thick as to be runny.

Over this coat of adhesive, sift the color you are using to counterenamel. See that it is spread evenly, with just a little more around the edges than in the center—as you covered the circular shape in the first project. Remember, always, that enamel has a tendency to burn away first around the edges of a piece, and thus must be a shade thicker at this point.

As in the earlier project, you may coat the face of the copper pieces with fire-scale retardant if you wish. Later, you will want to adopt the more professional method of acid cleaning between firings, at least for all pieces on which you are using acid-resistant colors. For now, the series of steps are simplified somewhat if you use the fire-scale retardant.

When the counterenamel has been sifted onto the pieces thoroughly, allow them to dry, then lift them gently with the spatula onto the Nichrome-mesh rack, and lift into the pre-heated kiln. It is not necessary to use the trivets this time, since there is no enamel on the second side of the pieces, and they will not stick to the rack.

Fire the counterenamel only until it has reached the dull, orange-peel stage—remembering that it will be fired at least two more times.

Remove the rack and copper pieces from the kiln at this point, and allow them to cool completely. The fire scale retardant will probably fall away in large flakes. Any that adheres may be removed easily with any improvised scraper—the back edge of a knife should do nicely. Just don't touch the surface of the copper with your hands or you'll have the cleaning to do all over again, and be careful not to scratch your copper—those scratches will show if you use transparent enamel.

Now place the cooled shapes on another clean piece of paper, counterenameled side down. Coat the face sides of the shapes with adhesive, just as you did the reverse sides. Then sift on the color you have chosen to use for the base coat. Again, remember to build the coat of enamel thicker around the edges than it is in the center.

After it has been dried, it is ready for firing. For this firing, however, the trivets are necessary. Each tiny circle is lifted carefully onto a trivet, resting either on the sides, or on the points, of the trivet. If it rests on the points, there will be minute pin-prick marks left in the counterenamel when the trivet is broken away after the firing. These marks are inconsequential in something like earrings or other objects where the reverse side is not seen.

The trivets are carefully lifted onto the Nichrome rack which is placed in the kiln for firing. Again, this firing will bring the enamel to the dull stage only. (Remember that there remains one more firing, at which time the glassy, glossy stage will be accomplished.)

The moment the orange-peel stage is reached, remove rack and contents from the kiln and allow to cool completely.

Once the base-coated pieces are completely cool, it is time to apply your design. Place the pieces on your white paper. Use a fine-pointed brush, dipping it in the adhesive to charge it sparingly, and draw your design onto the base color. Be careful that your hand does not touch the face of the piece during this step.

This is a bit tricky, until you've got the hang of it. You cannot trace your design onto the base coat with either carbon paper or pencil. Carbon paper leaves grease marks; graphite particles from the pencil would burn out and destroy your design. You could incise it lightly with a scriber, or any sharp-pointed instrument. But until you're more experienced at that sort of thing, the etched lines would probably show through on the finished piece. However, in a good light, you'll be able to see the lines you're drawing with the adhesive, and complete your design successfully.

Using the color you've chosen for the design, sift it carefully, and generously, over the entire face of the piece. Then, picking up the piece carefully with the tweezers, gently turn it at an angle, so that all the enamel not adhering to the adhesive has a chance to fall free, onto the clean paper.

Suddenly your design jumps out at you!

At this point you may spot gaps in a line, or places where a bit of touch-up seems called for. You may apply more adhesive carefully, sift on more enamel, again tap off the excess. So long as you do not touch the piece with your fingers, nor disturb the lines already drawn, you may continue this until the design looks right to you.

Once you reach the point where you feel you can't improve on the design, remove any grains remaining on the fired enamel with a brush which has been dipped in clean water. Replace the copper-plus-trivet on the Nichrome rack, and slide the whole business back in the kiln.

Now you'll leave it in the kiln until the entire surface reaches the glassy stage. And no longer! Don't run the risk of burning it out around the edges by letting it stay in the kiln "just a few seconds longer." The moment it turns glossy—out it comes!

Cooled again, all that remains is the final clean-up job, and fastening on the findings.

In this piece, as in the one in the preceding chapter, there will have been some fire-scale buildup around the edges. This fire scale may be cleaned away, and the copper exposed most attractively by using a fine file. Always remember to file from the edges downward—and in long, smooth strokes. If you use short, choppy jabs with the file, you'll net a ragged edge on your copper.

When the edges have been cleaned to your satisfaction, the earring backs may be fastened to the enameled copper. This joining may be done with epoxy glue. Or, if you have skipped the counterenameling step, the findings may be soldered to the bare, thoroughly cleaned copper with one of the low-fire solders. Using this process, a bit of solder is dabbed on the finding, it is held tight to the copper piece with a self-locking (or soldering) tweezers, and a lighted match is applied to the solder area. It flames out briefly, and *voilà*—the joining is accomplished. There are other, more complicated methods of joining findings and enameled pieces—but for the beginner either of those described accomplishes a neat and enduring joint easily and swiftly.

CHAPTER 6
TRY A STENCIL

YOU WILL NEED

1 copper shape—round or square, small enough to fit
   your kiln
80-mesh enamels—one light, one dark color
Adhesive
Sifter
Tongs
Small piece of cardboard (shirt boards are excellent)
Several clean paper towels
Small wooden box with recessed cover, made especially
   to accommodate enameled plaques
Lacquer or stain to finish box

This exercise in stenciling has been designed to acquaint you with the technique. Arbitrarily we have chosen to make a panel which will decorate the top of a small box. You may wish to proceed on some other project, adapting the technique as you go.

If you, too, are using the small wooden box, it is a good idea to have this either lacquered or stained, completely finished and dry before you begin work on your decorative enamel panel. And of course you have made sure that your copper plaque is the right size for the recess in your box cover.

While your kiln is heating, doodle a design on a scrap of paper the same size as your plaque. Experiment until you hit on something that pleases you. Because it is simple and uncomplicated, we have chosen a stylized leaf. Once decided upon, the design is transferred to lightweight cardboard, and cut out carefully with a razor blade or wood-carving knife.

When it is completed to your satisfaction, the leaf shape is carefully separated from the cardboard square. We won't use the leaf shape itself, but the hole it left, for our stencil. Don't throw away the leaf shape, however—start a file of stencil designs, for sometime you may want to use it in a reverse stencil design.

Fire the copper square following the same procedure used in the earlier projects, i.e., 1) cleaning; 2) counterenameling; 3) another cleaning; and 4) applying the base coat. Remember to use a trivet—or the counterenamel will stick to the Nichrome-mesh rack, ruining the counterenamel and the rack.

When the copper shape has been enameled on both sides, cut a duplicate of the leaf stencil from a piece of paper towel. Wet that towel stencil carefully—not soaking wet, but sufficiently damp so that it will cling to the enamel. Position it on the copper shape precisely where you want the leaf shape to appear. Ever so carefully, paint the exposed portion with adhesive, just as you would if you were stenciling a design with paint. Then sift an even coat of enamel over that exposed portion of the copper piece. Let it set for only a minute or two. The paper towel should not have a chance to dry out or it may stick to the copper piece. Gently lift it off the copper piece, and set the stencil aside on a clean piece of paper. (When it is completely dry, you will be able to shake off the excess enamel onto the clean paper, and return it to the vial.)

This first leaf design is then underfired, and allowed to cool.

Using another paper-towel stencil, made from the same cardboard master stencil, place another leaf on the copper square. Put it at right angles to the first leaf, or put it parallel, with edges slightly overlapping. Use a third color, and apply evenly but solidly, as you did the first leaf. Again underfire the piece to set the second leaf design.

From this point on you may want to ad-lib it. Perhaps a slight misting of one, or both, of the lighter colors can be scattered across the design, tying it all together. Perhaps you'll want to draw a few accent lines with a brush dipped in adhesive, then sift on a dark color for accent—tapping the excess enamel off onto a clean piece of paper and cleaning off stray particles with a damp brush. Then fire the whole piece again.

Say you've done the base coat in a rich brown, one leaf in orange, and the second in lime green. Try a yellow line here and there for accent. Make it absolutely, individually, your own design.

The final firing should fuse all the colors, and should be allowed to reach the glassy stage.

After the piece has cooled, the edges should be filed gently with emery cloth or a fine file, to remove any fire scale which has built up, and any irregularities along the edge of the enamel. Remember, always file away from the edge, not toward the center, of the piece.

Once the copper shape is cleaned and polished, you are ready to affix it to the little box. A good epoxy cement should do the job beautifully. Follow directions on the label of the cement you're using, and use it judiciously. Too much, and it will come creeping out around the edges. Too little, and you won't get a good bond. It might be a good idea to set the piece under a heavy weight (protecting the face of the enamel plate with several layers of tissue) while the cement is drying.

The stenciling process, you must agree, is simple and no drawing ability is necessary—try using natural forms for some of your stencils. On a base coat of dark green enamel, place a small section of fern, or an interesting leaf. Sift a coat of lighter green, or tan, or yellow, over the entire piece, then gently lift off the fern or leaf. You have the silhouette form of the natural object, more beautifully outlined than you could ever draw it. Or use an intricately cut lace paper doily as a stencil on a small round tray.

Half the fun of stenciling is in finding objects that lend their outlines to a decorative design. Get your imagination into high gear!

CHAPTER 7
GLASS LUMPS
AND
THREADS

YOU WILL NEED

1 copper shape
80-mesh enamel in desired base-coat color
Chunks and/or threads in either assorted colors, or de-
sired combination
Sifter
Tweezers
Usual kiln tools—trivet, rack, tongs, etc.

This project is another quickie—designed purely to acquaint you with the behavior in the kiln of both enamel
lumps and threads. It will also, we hope, spark your imagination as to the numberless ways you can go, using these bits
of glass to create dramatic decorative effects.

As in all preceding projects, the copper shape is cleaned thoroughly and dried, counterenameled, and then given a base coat in the desired color.

Then comes the fun. An even coat of adhesive is applied over the base coat—be careful that it is not too thick, or the lumps and threads may slither about. With the tweezers, small lumps of enamel are placed on the base coat wherever desired. You can try for a neat, orderly composition by placing similarly sized lumps in an evenly spaced border around the edge of a circular shape. Or you can go for the casual I-just-tossed-them-on effect, by using a variety of sizes and colors of lumps, placed in hit-or-miss fashion in the center of the piece.

And of course you may use the lumps as almost every enamelist does at one time or another early in his experience, creating a miniature version of an artist's palette. Stock shapes of the palette are available at most hobby shops. These are given a base coat of tan opaque enamel, then the lumps, in primary and secondary colors, are placed around the edges just as a painter would place his oils. It's a cliché project in enameling—but fun.

When the lumps have been arranged to your satisfaction, into the kiln goes the piece. Great care must be exercised here. Any undue jiggling, bumping or tilting of the copper piece might cause your careful composition to slide out of alignment.

Firing of the lumps must be watched carefully, and the piece removed immediately when the lumps have reached the desired stage. You may prefer the lumps barely melted, so they are just fused with the base coat. You may want them half-melted, so they form slightly raised places on the design. Or you may want to wait until the lumps are completely melted and puddled on the base coat. Your timing of the firing will depend upon what you want from the lumps.

If you are using threads, you may wish to take a few in the tweezers and drop them onto the piece in a casual jackstraw composition. Or, carefully plucking out the preferred colors from your assortment, you might compose a plaidlike pattern. Or rays radiating from a central point. There are ever so many things you can do with both lumps and threads.

One note of caution. If you are making two or more matched items—earrings, cuff links, links for a bracelet—be careful when selecting either lumps or threads in the dark colors. In the unfired state the dark blues and dark greens are often hard to differentiate from black. It might be a good idea to take one long glass thread in your tweezers, break it in two with another tweezers, and put half on each cuff link. That way you know the colors will match.

Remember, too, that any balanced design looks better reversed on the second earring or cuff link. If it's a hit-or-miss pattern, no studied reversal is necessary.

Using lumps and threads, either together or separately, can create a confettilike effect, and make for a lighthearted, informal sort of piece, suitable for any age or any decor.

CHAPTER 8
SGRAFFITO

YOU WILL NEED

1 copper shape—a small ashtray, 3" in diameter, or
   larger if your kiln accommodates
80-mesh enamels in two colors: one dark, one light
Sifter
Atomizer or brush for applying adhesive
Scriber, or any pointed instrument
Usual tools for kiln work: trivet, rack, tongs, etc.

This will be a two-fold exercise. Since the technique of
sgraffito, basically, is so simple in itself, we will also gain
some experience, in this exercise, with enameling three-
dimensional shapes.

Sgraffito is, literally, scratching. A layer of fired enamel is covered with a contrasting layer of enamel, and the design is then scratched away, uncovering the base coat. A second firing sets the design.

But, before we can play around with this new technique, there must be the routine operations which precede any project. The copper shape is thoroughly cleaned. With the ashtray upside down on a clean piece of paper, spray on an even coat of adhesive. It is possible to paint on this coat with a brush, but the atomizer will give you a much smoother, more even coat. Then sift on an even coat of enamel, making sure there are no thin spots, and none too thickly covered. If you want the base of the ashtray, which will rest on the table, to remain copper, you must mask it off during this part of the procedure. Place a paper disc, cut to fit precisely, over the base before you sift on the enamel. Lift this off most carefully just before the piece is fired.

After the enamel has dried, place the piece carefully on the Nichrome-mesh rack, set it into the preheated kiln, and fire only to the orange-peel stage.

When the piece is removed from the kiln and cooled, you will want to check it carefully to make sure no bubbles have appeared, and that all areas are completely covered. It may be necessary to patch a few spots, and fire a second time before continuing.

When the bottom side of the ashtray is enameled to your satisfaction, you may proceed with the top side. Clean off the fire scale by whatever method (described earlier) you have found you prefer.

Coat the top surface, again with an atomizer if possible, evenly with adhesive. Not too thickly, though—if you put on too much, it will run and puddle at the bottom of your tray.

If you put it on too sparingly, you may end up with bare patches of metal.

On top of the adhesive, sift the base-coat color. We would choose one of the off-white shades, with a blue tint to it. Fire this as you did the reverse side—with one exception. This time the ashtray must be put on a trivet before it is placed on the Nichrome rack.

When the piece has been removed from the kiln and cooled, cover the base-coat enamel with adhesive, and sift on the contrasting color. We might use a blue-sapphire or Dresden or ultramarine. This coat may be sifted only in the center, shading off toward the edges. Or it may coat the piece completely.

While this coat of enamel is still moist from the adhesive beneath it, take the scriber and scratch through the top coat, exposing the color beneath. You should have already sketched out your design on paper—this is no time to ad-lib. Follow that design.

Let it dry, then spray it again, gently, with adhesive, to set any stray granules of color. A word of caution—do not be too exuberant in this final spraying step or you'll be blowing the enamel right off the tray!

When the whole piece has dried, fire it—this time to the glassy stage.

Then all that remains is the cooling, and the final cleaning operation, filing the edges and smoothing them with emery cloth.

As you attempt other sgraffito pieces, you will want to experiment—and there are zillions of ways to go. Eliminate the opaque base coat—scratch your design into a color which has been sprinkled over a coat of clear flux, so that the copper itself gleams through. Try intricate designs with two colors not so markedly contrasting—you can get gloriously subtle effects that way.

And a very practical use we have seen for sgraffito—particularly adaptable if you pride yourself on your printing ability—is nameplates. An oblong copper plate, one or two inches wide and as long as you need for the name you're printing, is drilled with a small hole in either end. This plate is covered first with a dark color, and fired. Then the lighter second coat is dusted on, and the name scratched through it, neatly and legibly. (Of course, the colors could be reversed—dark on light—that's your option.) When this is fired, it results in a door nameplate deluxe, which should be a wonderful gift for newlyweds or a couple just moved into their first home.

CHAPTER 9
SWIRLING

YOU WILL NEED

1 copper shape—3" diameter circle
Small wooden box, somewhat larger than 3" diameter
(Note: if your kiln accommodates larger pieces, dimen-
   sions may be increased as you wish)
80-mesh enamels—one color for base coat
Enamel lumps—two or three colors in pleasant harmony
   with base coat
Swirling tool
Asbestos glove
Nichrome-mesh rack, trivet, spatula, tongs

Some call it swirling, some call it scrolling. Whatever ter-
minology you decide on, this is a technique that approaches

abstract art in feeling. It is free, flowing, and dramatic. Depending on the color harmonies involved, it can be lively and lighthearted, or it can be cool, placid, and moody.

A base-coat color is fired on your copper shape, using the method described in earlier chapters. You may elect to eliminate the counterenamel on this piece, since it is to be cemented flat onto a box top. However, for pieces larger than the three-inch circle, counterenamel is still a good idea, to guard against warping.

When the piece has cooled after the base-coat firing, a coat of adhesive is applied. Be extra careful that this is not too thick, or the lumps will slide and slither out of position. Using tweezers, place lumps of glass in selected colors at the desired spots on the piece. Perhaps you will want to place these evenly around the border of the piece, or at random in the center. Use only two or three colors. Until you've mastered the technique, more than three colors can end up looking like someone had dropped the paint pot.

With the lumps in place in the desired spots, the piece is placed on a trivet, then on the Nichrome-mesh rack, and into the kiln. Now comes the tricky part.

Be sure you're wearing an asbestos glove. An oven mitt will work well, if it isn't too bulky. The moment the surface of the enamel begins to level out, and the orange-peel stage is reached, start stirring. If the lumps have been clustered in the center of the piece, a simple stir or two with the tool will be sufficient. If they have been spotted around the border, you may wish to use a second swirling tool to rotate the copper piece, still in the kiln, as you give a quick swish through each puddle of color with the swirling tool in your right hand. Don't overdo it, however. Too much stirring will result in a muddy hodgepodge of color.

Ultimately, as you master the technique, you will find that you can control the effects rather easily. Rhythmic circular motions around the edge of the piece will result in a garland of scrolls and arabesques more graceful than most artists could execute with a pen or brush. One studio-produced tray we've seen was done on a white base coat, with scrolling in red and two shades of blue around its circumference—and it looked precisely like bunting flying in the breeze on the Fourth of July.

Depending upon where you spot the enamel lumps, and the pattern of your swirling strokes, you create an enormous variety of designs. The tightness or looseness of your swirling strokes, the colors you are using—all will have an effect on the ultimate mood of your design.

This is truly the technique for anyone sensitive to the mood-producing effects of color. Swirls of red, orange and yellow in the center of a shallow copper bowl give the impression that the whole piece is on fire. Neat little scrolls of aquamarine and larkspur on a darker blue base evoke the feeling of rain dropping into a quiet pool. The effects that can be achieved are infinite.

CHAPTER 10
CHAMPLEVÉ

YOU WILL NEED

Stock copper shapes
Etching mordant
Asphalt paint, or asphaltum varnish
Oblong glass baking dish
80-mesh enamels
Fine-pointed brushes
Gum tragacanth
Pointed instrument
Earring or cuff-link findings
Epoxy cement

Champlevé (shawm-pleh-VAY) is an impressive-sounding technique. It produces impressive objects, even in the hands of amateurs.

Hundreds of years ago, craftsmen chiseled and gouged and scribed designs into metal, then filled the resulting depressions with enamels, and fired the object.

Today the craftsman has an infinitely faster and easier way to obtain the same results; those metals may now be etched in minutes to get the same design effect it would have taken days to reach with a hammer and chisel.

Basically, champlevé starts with the etching process. The desired design is etched into the copper, the resulting depressions in the metal are filled with enamel and fired. The result is an exciting contrast between exposed bright metal and colored inserts.

The shape you chose to enamel will depend on your own whim. Butterflies and fish are fun to do in champlevé. These are available in stock shapes, in eighteen-gauge copper.

As in every enameling project, the metal is cleaned thoroughly before any of the other work is begun. The asphalt paint will not adhere properly to a greasy or oily surface.

When you are confident that the copper is thoroughly clean and dry, paint the back and all edges with the asphalt paint. As in earlier projects—do not handle the copper with your bare hands. Hold it with the tongs, or with cleaned tweezers, during the painting. Allow the paint to dry before working on the face of the piece. The drying may take several hours.

While the asphalt paint is drying, make a *sketch* which will be your guide for painting the face of the piece. Make your sketch the same size as your copper piece, and decide where the dividing lines will go. Remember that every surface you cover with the asphalt paint will remain bright copper in the finished piece. The exposed areas will be etched away by the acid. Paint the lines boldly—but not too broadly. And resist the temptation to make the design too detailed. Larger areas of color, with their bandings of copper, are infinitely more effective than tiny spots. And certainly there is no need to keep to natural effects. Let your imagination run wild. There may not be many butterflies in green and purple in nature—but they can be very eye-filling in enameled copper.

Once the back and edges of the asphalt-painted shapes have dried, take a fine-pointed brush, and using your color sketch as a guide, paint the dividing lines on the top surface of your copper piece with the asphalt paint. Divide the colored areas of the wings, if it's a butterfly—or the lines of scales, if it's a fish.

If any bubbles appear in the asphalt, either on the backing or on the face design, carefully break them and repaint that area. If this is not done, the thin, bubbled area of the asphalt paint will allow etching in spots where you hadn't planned any etching. If the lines you've painted aren't sharp enough to suit you, let them dry somewhat, then straighten them up, using an Exacto-knife, or even a single-edged razor blade.

Again, the asphalt-painted face design must be thoroughly dry before being submerged in the etching bath.

Prepare the etching mordant as directed on the label. Some solutions work better when warm—not hot. If the glass tray with the solution could be placed on an electric trivet set at the lowest heat, this would be ideal. Some solutions take several hours to etch to the required depth, others take less than an hour. The label on the etching mordant you buy should give you a clue to its speed. Generally the slower-working etchers give a cleaner line because they break up the copper particles with less turbulence.

When you have acquired more confidence in your ability to handle the copper during the etching process, you may wish to switch from the commercially prepared mordants to the process used by professionals—a nitric acid solution. Most craftsmen use a solution of one part nitric acid and three parts water. And remember, always—*acid is poured into water,* never vice versa. Acid should not touch the skin and the fumes it gives off during the etching process are dangerous. If you decide to use it, exercise caution.

During the etching process, check periodically on the progress, using the tongs to lift the piece from its bath. Any tiny bubbles which form during the etching should be gently dispersed with a swab or a feather. Left undisturbed, they would pit the surface of the copper. Many craftsmen prefer to do the etching with the copper plate face-down in the solution, so that any grains of copper loosened from the plate may fall to the bottom of the tray, and not impede the remaining etching process.

When the exposed portion of the plate has been etched to the desired depth (approximately one-half the thickness of the copper), the plate may be removed from the solution, using the tongs. It should then be rinsed thoroughly under cold running water. Check the label on your etching mordant for information about storage and future use of the remaining solution.

The asphalt paint may now be removed from the copper. Use turpentine and a soft cloth for this job. A final thorough cleaning, and you are ready to color the piece.

It is best to counterenamel any flat pieces. The variation in the depth of the face of the piece may cause it to warp in the firing if you skip the counterenamel. Use a very thin coat of counterenamel.

If your shop stocks them, buy enamels ground finer than 80-mesh for this job. If these finer enamels are too difficult to obtain, you can make-do with the 80-mesh. Mix a small amount of the enamel with a drop or two of gum tragacanth into a pastelike consistency. Glass caster cups, such as those used under heavy furniture, are perfect miniature mixing bowls for this step.

With the sharp point of a clean brush, pick up bits of the wet enamel and deposit it in the depressions made by the etching. Follow the color sketch you completed earlier. The color is built up inside each little "pen" until it is heaped somewhat higher than the surrounding metal. During the firing it will shrink and level out. If there are any corners into which it is difficult to pack the color with the brush, use a sharp pointed instrument or toothpick. Poke the corners solidly full of color.

The toothpick comes in handy, too, to pick up any stray bits of enamel that may have escaped onto the clear portion of the copper design.

When all the depressions have been charged with color, set the piece aside to dry. Fired wet, the moisture still in the enamel-tragacanth mixture would steam and explode, ruining your piece and possibly even your kiln.

Once it is dry, the piece may be fired the same as those described earlier. If you were very skillful, or just plain lucky, the areas of color were built to the correct height, and will be flush with the exposed copper after the firing. Chances are, however, that each tiny pen of color will show a slight depression in its center, which must be filled. Another firing follows. It may even be necessary to put the piece through three or more firings.

When the enamel portions of your design have been built up to your satisfaction, it is time to give the piece its final polishing. The fire scale may be removed with a brief bath in the pickling solution. The vinegar-salt bath has no effect on the enamels. The fire scale thus removed, a gentle buffing with metal polish and a soft cloth will bring the piece to its full beauty.

Depending on its function, you will now affix to the back either the earring or cuff-link findings. There are any number of methods you can follow to join the two. We prefer to use a good grade of epoxy cement. Or you could try a good all-purpose craft glue, a liquid solder, or a solder that melts when flamed by a match. You will soon hit on the method with which you are most comfortable.

At this point the earrings or cuff links on which you have been working could be worn. Many craftsmen, however, prefer to protect the metal portion of their creations with a very thin coat of colorless, clear plastic which may be brushed on. It dries quite rapidly.

You are now ready to wear the jewelry you have made, or to present it as a gift. Be prepared to collect compliments.

CHAPTER 11
CLOISONNÉ

YOU WILL NEED

1 copper piece in desired shape
80-mesh enamels in desired colors
Adhesive for moistening colors
One package silver cloissoné wire
Brushes
Wet inlay tools, one for spreading, one for lifting and
    placing enamels
Tweezers
Round-nose pliers
Adhesive solution
Usual tools for cleaning and firing procedures

Cloisonné, in which the enamel is set in hollows formed by thin strips of wire, is probably the oldest technique used in enameling. In ancient times, craftsmen must have felt it necessary to build separate little pens to hold each color of molten enamel. It is only in comparatively recent examples of enameling that we find other techniques being used.

It is also one of the most spectacularly effective of the enameling techniques. And it isn't difficult, really. If you approach it sensibly and without trying to recreate some of the intricate oriental designs, you should master it easily. If you keep your design simple and uncomplicated, even your very first piece should be a smashing success.

Design, in fact, is all—in cloisonné. None of the casual, slapdash, almost unplanned effects of scrolling here. Each line, each tiny spot of color must work. And it is purely due to lack of planning that most beginners fail in their first few cloisonné pieces.

There is a trap to be avoided. Learning this may help you turn out successful pieces from the very first. Customarily, the planned design is laid out on paper. The various color areas are decided upon and the dividing lines, or cloisons, are indicated in bold black lines. Everything looks great. The design works. Then it is reproduced in enamels—and it falls apart.

On paper, there was a bold, dramatic design. On the enamel piece there are just so many spots of color. What the beginner failed to take into consideration was that the areas of color on the finished piece would not be tied together with bold, black lines—but by narrow, nearly white lines. And that can make all the difference.

Therefore, once you have a design figured out, make your final working sketch of it using pale gray separating lines—not those bold black ones. If the design still holds together, go on with the enamel. If it does not, replan your design.

But only when you do have a design that you feel will translate successfully into cloisonné should you proceed.

The first step is to anneal the silver wire, making it easier to cut and to bend. Coil the wire tightly, so that it fits into your kiln. Bind it securely for easier handling—use stainless-steel wire or a short length of the silver itself. Place the coil of wire on a Nichrome-mesh rack and into the kiln. Allow it to remain until it reaches a pink shade. Then remove it immediately, using the tongs, and plunge it into a pan of water. It will now be soft and malleable.

Holding the wire with tweezers and pliers (never with your hands), bend it to conform to the lines of your design, cutting it in appropriate lengths. Because it is oblong in shape, it will not stand upright by itself. Each tiny length must include some slight curve or angle. Only then will it remain upright during the firing.

When all the lengths of cloisonné wire have been cut and bent to shape, it is time to recreate your design on the actual copper piece, which you have already cleaned, counter-enameled, and enameled with its base coat.

If your design is simple—as a beginning design should be—you should have no difficulty setting the wires into their required positions without any guidelines.

However, if you feel you must have guidelines on the enamel base, lightly trace the required lines with a soft pencil. Then go over the pencil lines with a sharp-pointed scribe, barely scratching the surface of the enamel. Next, you must carefully remove all the graphite left by the pencil. A soft tissue or lintless cloth should do the trick. Moisten it slightly if necessary since any specks of graphite left behind will burn through the enamel and ruin your design. But by scribing the surface, you will have a guideline for placement of the silver wire.

Coat the enameled piece generously with adhesive solution. Lifting the wires with the tweezers, one at a time, carefully put them in place. You may have to do a bit of jockeying here and there, to move pieces so that corners meet properly and wires do not slide too closely together.

Once the wires are all in place, and the adhesive has dried, the piece may be fired. As the surface of the enamel melts, the wires sink in, and are firmly positioned. If you want to place the wires on bare copper, position them as described, then sift a generous coat of clear flux over the piece, allow all to dry, and fire. The flux, melting around the wires, will secure them.

When the piece is removed from the kiln, cooled, and any necessary cleaning done, you are ready to apply the colors. Small amounts of enamel are mixed with adhesive. The old-fashioned heavy glass caster cups make perfect little mixing bowls for this stage. The colors are now packed into the proper little pens, following your design. Since the enamel has a tendency to contract during the firing, it is a good idea to mound the enamels slightly in each little pen.

A word of caution here. Be sure that your tools are thoroughly cleaned each time you change colors. One speck of yellow showing up on a blue area in the finished piece could destroy the whole effect.

This is the stage where the tiny little wet inlay tools really justify their cost. Using them as you would a miniature shovel and a miniature hoe, you can handle the wet enamel with precision. The tiny shovel lifts enamel from the mixing bowl, and drops it into the cloisonné pen. The little hoe helps you push the wet enamel just where you want it, into corners, and up against the silver wire.

When you have finished with all the colors, the piece may be fired. You have probably used medium-fusing enamels throughout the piece, since these are the ones most readily available to the home craftsman. Therefore they will mature—or melt—at the same time. Be careful not to overfire.

When the piece has been removed from the kiln and cooled, you may find that many of the areas show small depressions in the center. There is nothing wrong with leaving it this way, if it pleases you. But the classic cloisonné has a smooth, even surface. To obtain this, simply fill each small depression with more enamel, and give the piece another firing.

If, after the second (or the third or fourth) firing, the level of the enamel has been brought up too far, so that it forms little mounds between the wires, that is easily taken care of.

When it has cooled completely, submerge the piece in a big pan of water—or hold it under running water—with one hand. With the other hand, apply the carborundum stone in steady, even strokes, until the entire surface is smooth. This may take a bit of time and patience, but the piece you are making will last for generations. The few extra minutes you spend in perfecting it will seem inconsequential.

After the stoning process, the enamels will have a dull, or matte, finish. Some craftsmen prefer to leave them that way. If you like a glossy piece, dry yours completely, then return it to the kiln just long enough to bring it back to the glossy stage.

There remain, of course, the finishing procedures of filing and polishing the edges. Some craftsmen like to finish off a piece of cloisonné by firing one thin coat of transparent flux over the whole piece. This is a protection and often deepens the colors dramatically—but it is purely optional.

Looking at your finished cloisonné, remember that many of the oriental-cloisonné pieces now on display were made several hundred years ago. Try to imagine what some descendant of yours will have to say about your cloisonné in the year 2272.

CHAPTER 12
PLIQUE-A-JOUR

If you have mastered the technique of cloisonné, then you should have no real problems in going on to plique-a-jour. Essentially, plique-a-jour is cloisonné without the copper backing—transparent so the light of day (*a jour*) passes through.

The Japanese and Chinese craftsmen of a century and more ago created plique-a-jour bowls and vases which are now museum pieces—or selling in the hundreds of dollars at antique shops. Their efforts could be duplicated today, by anyone with time and patience. The oriental craftsmen used a thin shell of copper, building up the design on its outer surface much in the manner of cloisonné. After firing, the bowl or vase was filled with acid, the inner shell of copper etched away, leaving only the transparent and translucent enamels supported by their maze of tiny cloison wires. This is a technique requiring not only patience and skill, but knowledge of the etching process. It is not a project for a beginner. But the dream of turning out such a piece is enough of a challenge to spur a beginner into becoming a pro.

And plique-a-jour, in its simplified form, just isn't all that difficult!

Many books on enameling do not even mention plique-a-jour. Or, if they do, they make it sound so complex as to frighten off the beginning enamelist. This is sad because plique-a-jour is not really complicated, but it is certainly one of the most dramatic techniques in enameling.

There are several ways to approach the plique-a-jour process. Each involves the creation of a design involving small apertures that will be filled with transparent enamels.

This design may be formed with wire, just as in cloisonné work. In the case of plique-a-jour, slightly heavier wire is used. Bezel wire, obtainable at hobby stores which stock silver jewelry-making supplies, is the general favorite. The design should be kept starkly simple, the apertures small. The impact here comes not from line, but from color, and the light transmitted through that color.

Once the design has been sketched in bold, black lines, the bezel wire is cut and bent to conform to those lines. It is secured with IT solder, used sparingly. IT solder is the hardest used on silver—any softer solder would melt in the kiln as the enamels are being fired.

When the silver filigree is completed, it is placed on a sheet of mica, and that in turn on a small section of fire brick. Make sure that the bottom edges of the wire filigree are snugly flush with the mica at all points. The apertures are then packed with either transparent glass lumps (the same sort you've used in swirling and scrolling) or with moistened 80-mesh transparent enamels. The lumps seem to give a better result, and many find them easier to work with. If 80-mesh enamels are used, they should be washed well first, to remove all cloudiness.

Each little silver pen should be completely filled. If you are using the lumps, fill the pens flush with the top of the bezel wire. If it is 80-mesh enamel you're using, mound it slightly in the center, just as you would for cloisonné. The finer enamel has a tendency to creep up the sides of the wires. Should this happen to your work to the point where small holes remain in the center of each aperture—no cause for alarm. Simply pack the hole full of more enamel and fire again.

Firing for either lumps or powdered enamel should be fast and hot. Watch the piece closely, and be prepared to remove it from the kiln the moment the surface levels out and turns glossy. Transparent enamels burn out easily, and you don't want to risk overfiring.

There may be a slight film of mica adhering to the bottom side of the piece once it is cooled and removed from its stand. This can be removed easily and rapidly with the carborundum stone, under running water. If the gloss has been affected, the piece can be returned to the kiln momentarily. This time its position should be reversed—what was the bottom side during the first firing now becomes the top side. If this is done only briefly, and in a very hot kiln—flash fired, as it were—the side that has just been stoned will regain its gloss, but the other side will not have a chance to pick up any mica particles.

Another method of creating the filigree for plique-a-jour is to use solid sheet silver in the size and shape desired, and to saw out the tiny openings. After the design has been sketched onto the silver, a hole is punched through the center of each aperture area, a saw inserted, and the aperture outlines carefully trimmed away. Of course, you will need to clean the piece thoroughly when all the sawing is completed—clean the edges of any rough projections by filing, and clean the metal itself in the acid bath.

If you are using the flat metal, it is a good idea to leave "ears," or projections, at regular intervals around the edge. When the metal is placed on the mica, and then on the fire brick, these small extensions can be used as anchor points, with stainless-steel brads pushed into the fire brick over each small "ear." Thus the flat metal shape is held snugly and securely to the mica mat.

The apertures in the flat metal are now filled in the same manner you would use in a cloisonné or champlevé piece. Use either transparent lumps or moistened, well-washed 80-mesh transparent enamels. Make an even layer of the lumps, or heap the 80-mesh enamel slightly in the center.

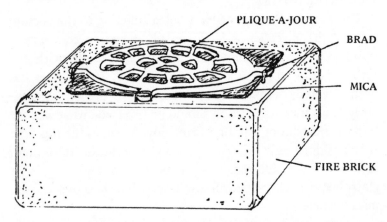

Fig. 11
Plique-a-jour anchored to fire brick

This, too, should be fired fast and hot.

When all the apertures have been filled to your satis-faction, and when the piece has been fired, removed from the kiln, and cooled—only then do you remove the brads anchor-ing it to the fire brick. If necessary, put the piece through the same stoning and refiring procedure described earlier to attain gloss on both sides.

In the finishing steps for the piece, you will want to saw off the small ears, file the edges, and give the piece an overall polish with a felt buffer and rouge. Be very careful, when cutting or sawing, not to flex or bend your project as this will pop out the enamel.

Traditionally, plique-a-jour was used for fine jewelry. It was a special favorite for earrings, which would hang free and thus allow the light to pass through. The technique has also been used most effectively in processional crosses, where the artisan's creation became, actually, a mobile stained-glass window.

In modern usage, plique-a-jour pendants could be em-ployed dramatically as window-shade pulls, catching the sun-light and transmitting colored patterns into a room. Or a plique-a-jour medallion might be used as a combined spot of color and warning signal cemented onto a sliding glass door. Or it could be pure decoration placed on a sunny window.

Just don't waste any plique-a-jour piece by placing it where no light can pass through.

CHAPTER 13

BASSE-TAILLE, GRISAILLE, AND EN RESILLE

The various techniques of enameling go on and on. Beyond the ones we have already explored—those which are suitable for the beginner's level of skill—there are many more which are infinitely more demanding of expertise.

BASSE-TAILLE

In basse-taille, for instance, the craftsman must be adept at metal work as well as enameling. A design is raised on the metal, creating a bas-relief-type picture or ornament. This is done through an elaborate process involving chasing tools, gouges, chisels, and a pitch block—all too intricate for a beginner to consider.

When the ornamentation in the metal is complete, the metal is cleaned, and layer after layer after layer of transparent enamel applied, until just the right tinting and subtle color shading is achieved. The heavier deposits of the transparent enamels in the crevices of the design heighten the three-dimensional effect.

GRISAILLE

Grisaille pieces are generally to be seen only in museums, and appropriately so. The technique calls for patience and skill, which are museum pieces in themselves these days.

On a dark base coat, three-dimensional figures are built up in multiple layers, through multiple firings, using only whites and shades of gray. When completed, the piece resembles an ivory carving set on onyx.

EN RESILLE

Also strictly in the museum-piece category is the en resille process. For this, designs were etched into plates of rock crystal. The etched lines were filled with gold, and that gold extended ever so slightly above the face of the crystal. Then the spaces between the gold lines were filled with finely ground soft-fusing enamels. The firing of these delicate objects must have been an extremely critical operation. But those which came whole from the kiln, and now rest in their museum showcases, are wondrous to behold.

It is highly unlikely that the amateur will even want to progress to the point where he can turn out a basse-taille piece, or one in grisaille. But when you're working in any medium, it is exciting and stimulating to know just how many applications of that medium are available, and to contemplate what could be done if you only had the time.

Knowing about these involved techniques will help you to recognize them when you come upon them in museum examples.

And it is such fun to drop these elegant sounding terms into casual conversations—especially with a layman who thinks he's enameling when he slaps a coat of paint on Junior's tricycle.

CHAPTER 14
USING GOLD AND SILVER FOIL

YOU WILL NEED

1 copper shape
80-mesh enamels—opaque or transparent for base coat,
    transparent for use over foil
1 piece gold or silver foil
Brush
Adhesive
Scissors
Piercing tool (explanation below)

With the use of metallic foil, fired under transparent
enamels, some of the most flamboyant and dramatic designs
imaginable can be created. It is not a technique to be at-
tempted by the all-thumbs set. But presumably any crafts-

man in enamels has developed a degree of manual dexterity and should be able to handle the tricky foil with a little practice.

Foil is not cheap. A small square, about half the size of a postal card, in silver, will cost approximately fifty cents. In gold, a square only slightly larger will probably cost several dollars.

With this cost factor in mind, you will want to plan your design very carefully and have the procedure clearly in mind. You will want to do everything right the first time around, on this one. Goofs can be expensive.

When planning your design, keep in mind that the silver foil shows up to best advantage when used under cool transparent enamels—shades of blue and green. Gold foil adds dramatic fire to warm colors—shades of yellow ranging through orange to the reds and on into the browns. If it is flower or leaf shapes you are using in your design, remember these color affinities.

Once your design has been decided upon, it is time to do the preparatory firing of your copper piece. Fire the counterenamel and the base coat in the manner described in earlier chapters. Depending on your design, your base coat may be an opaque color, or a transparent. Only when the piece has cooled should you cut the foil shapes.

Having determined just what design you will follow, you know what areas will be punched up with foil. Place a sheet of artist's tracing paper (the thin, almost transparent white paper—*not* carbon paper) over your design, and trace the shapes of those areas which are to be covered with foil. Cut out these shapes most carefully, using sharp scissors. These cutouts will be the patterns you use when cutting the foil.

Foil comes packaged between sheets of tissue. It must remain between those tissues at all times—until the zero hour when you transfer it to your copper piece. Never touch it with your fingers.

The pattern you have cut from tracing paper is now retraced onto the top sheet of tissue surrounding the foil. Plan here, too, so that in cutting there will be a minimum amount of waste.

Holding the "sandwich" of tissue-foil-tissue firmly between thumb and forefinger, cut around your traced line with a good, sharp scissors. When you have all the foil parts of your design cut and ready, if you must put them aside temporarily, be sure to weight them. A chance breeze could scatter them easily, and disastrously.

If the foil piece or pieces you have cut are large, they should be pricked with many minute holes, to allow air trapped beneath to escape during the firing. If you fail to do this, you may end up with a lovely big metallic bubble right in the middle of your design.

To do the pricking job rapidly and evenly, fashion a piercing tool of your own from a large cork and a package of needles. Stick the needles—a dozen or more of them—head-first into the cork. Push them in securely and, at the same time, line up the points evenly by pushing the cork against a hard, smooth surface.

Just before you place the foil on the copper, puncture the sandwich—tissue-foil-tissue—with this multineedled tool, so that the entire surface of the foil shape is covered with tiny holes.

With a brush, cover the base-coated enamel piece with adhesive. Then, with the wet brush, carefully lift the top layer of tissue off the foil and place it to one side. Again with the wet brush, lift the foil shape and place it in the proper position on the enamel. Repeat this process for all the foil pieces you are using. Be careful, too, that you haven't inadvertently transferred the bottom layer of tissue along with the foil onto the enameled piece.

Now, carefully and gently, make sure that the foil is flat and smooth—tamping it down ever so lightly with a blotter or a clean tissue to remove excess moisture.

The entire piece is now covered once more with adhesive. It is really better to spray on this coat if possible, since the use of a brush might possibly dislodge the foil from its planned location. Then a thin, but even, coat of transparent enamel is sifted over all. Later you may wish to experiment with the effects you can get by varying the thickness of your transparent enamels. For the beginning, it's better to learn to get it on evenly.

After the piece has had a chance to dry, it is fired—to the glassy stage.

Some craftsmen prefer to reach this point in two stages. They use a firing after the foil has been set onto the enamel, and a second after the transparent enamel has been sifted over. There is a danger here, however, that the foil will burn. And there must be a polishing step between, with the foil being burnished back to its original brightness after the first firing. This introduces still another danger of damaging the foil. By firing the transparent enamels directly onto the foil, these dangers are eliminated, and one complete step avoided.

It is possible to use the foil without a base coat of enamel. A coat of clear flux is fired over the copper, the foil adhered to this, and the transparent enamels sifted over all. This is particularly effective in a design that combines the bright raw copper color with gold foil and transparent enamels in shades of orange and red. Colors almost blaze forth from such a piece.

There are no "thou shalt nots" in composing for enamel pieces. What one craftsman may consider impossible, another may accomplish with ease. One museum-quality bowl, the image of which lingers in the memory, demonstrates the point. It could have symbolized fire and ice—one side employed silver foil beneath subtle shades of blue through aqua to green, the other side was blazing with gold foil and raw copper, under red and orange transparent glazes.

This is half the fun of enameling—experimenting with the effects one can get—and daring to do something no one else may have tried before.

A word of economy here. Whenever you use foil, tenderly save all the scraps, between their layers of tissue, and keep them stored carefully in a clean envelope. Put that envelope between cardboards to prevent its being crumpled. Even the tiniest shards of foil can be used, ultimately, to add sparkle to some design. Therefore, though the initial price of the foil may seem a bit steep, one sheet can be used to add excitement to a number of enameled pieces.

CHAPTER 15
CUT AND SHAPE YOUR OWN

Most enamelists reach the point, sooner or later, where they want to "make something from scratch." It is true that there are myriads of shapes available to enamelists. Flat shapes, and formed pieces, big and little, square, round, and freeform. But the craftsman begins to feel like a gourmet chef faced with too many TV dinners. He feels the challenge to create something from the very beginning—not just pick it up halfway through and finish it.

It is at this point that the craftsman is ready to cut and form his own bowl or tray, or whatever. This can open the door to a whole new craft, one that dovetails beautifully with the already learned art of enameling.

Since our craftsman intends to enamel the piece once he's shaped it, he must keep the dimensions within the limitations of his kiln. Let us say he decides to make a small, shallow bowl, about six inches in diameter—an excellent choice for a first adventure in shaping.

You can buy a stock copper disc in this size, and start with that. But in doing so, you would eliminate one of the steps in "creating from scratch." Instead, buy a seven-inch square of eighteen-gauge copper.

First step in the process is to anneal the metal. It is placed in a hot kiln and heated to the cherry-red point. Removed from the kiln with the tongs, it is immediately plunged into a bucket of cold water. It is now more malleable, more easily cut and bent.

Drawing diagonal lines from corner to corner, find the center of the piece where those diagonals intersect. With the scriber inserted in a compass, draw a circle of approximately six and a half inches. A shade more, or a shade less, won't matter.

Then, with a pair of good metal shears, cut the blank into a circle shape. Do not do this with one long looping cut, however. First remove the corner portions of the square, cutting close to the line you have just drawn, but not on it. Then, following the circle you have drawn for only short distances, cut off on a tangent from that circle, removing all unwanted portions of the copper.

The cutting job should be done slowly and carefully. The more smoothly the cut is made, the less filing is necessary later. It is a good idea to wear gloves—the sharp edges of the freshly cut copper can give a nasty cut or scratch.

When the circle has been cut to your satisfaction, it is time to start the pounding that will turn this flat disc into a pleasantly rounded bowl.

To help in the shaping process, secure a piece of hardwood—something about 4 x 4 and six inches long would serve. This hardwood block is secured tightly in the workbench with the grain end up. With a ball peen hammer, pound a curved depression into the grain end of the hardwood.

Some craftsmen find it helps to mark the copper disc in concentric circles, using a china marking pencil or felt-tip pen, before they start the beating process. These marks serve as a guide, and make for a more even pattern in the "raising."

The edge of the copper disc is laid against the depression in the hardwood block, and the beating is started, using the rounded end of a ball peen hammer or a "raising" hammer. Do not strike the very edge of the copper. Begin the strokes just inside the edge. Rotate the disc evenly as the blows are struck, and make one complete circuit of the disc before shifting to the next lower pattern of circles. Keep the blows even and overlapping slightly—the edge of one hammer blow should barely lap the edge of the preceding blow.

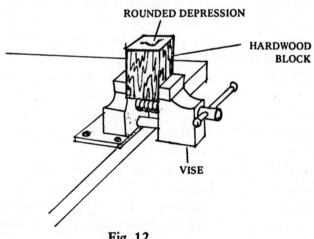

Fig. 12
Hardwood shaping block

Even as you finish the first circle of hammer blows, you will see the disc taking on shape. It will be necessary to anneal the copper periodically, as it stiffens and hardens under the repeated beating. Authorities recommend that annealing be done once for every quarter-inch in depth reached in the shaping.

After you have followed the pattern of concentric circles completely to the center, you will probably find that the bowl is not yet as deep as you want it to be. Simply anneal it again, and repeat the procedure until the desired depth has been attained.

If certain areas of the bowl seem to have flattened out, you may alter them with a few short, sharp blows with your hammer. If there are indentations too deep to suit you at other points, simply invert the bowl on the stake, and strike out the offending bumps, using a wooden or rawhide mallet.

Don't be timid about annealing the copper as often as you feel is necessary. If the copper is raised too rapidly, without annealing, it may crack.

When the bowl is finally the shape you want (this will take longer than it sounds on paper), it is time to do the cleaning and planishing (toughening and polishing by hammering lightly). The copper should be pickled—using the same nitric-acid and water solution you would use for cleaning any other copper piece. Any stubborn spots of fire scale should be removed with steel wool.

A planishing stake as near the same curve as the bowl should be placed in the vise. Its surface, and the surface of the planishing hammer you use, should be mirror smooth. The purpose of the planishing process is to compact the metal, make it harder and more durable, and to bring it to a fine polish.

With the bowl inverted over the planishing stake, you will start at the center, striking light, firm blows with the planishing hammer. Rotate the bowl on the stake so that the blows follow a pattern of concentric circles outward toward the edge. This time the blows should not overlap, but barely touch. The planishing creates facets on the surface of the bowl, and these should be evenly spaced for best effect.

Make sure the hammer blows always hit the metal precisely at the point where it is resting on the planishing stake. Otherwise, you will collect some gorgeous dents to be laboriously removed. Normally, you should not find it necessary to do any annealing during the planishing process since you are no longer shaping the metal, only firming it.

In order for the finished bowl to rest safely on a flat surface, you must now flatten its base. This job is done only after the planishing has been completed.

A bottoming stake of the desired dimensions is selected. A circle of that dimension is marked on the inside of the bowl. The bowl is then placed on a sandbag, the bottoming stake held firmly in place against the marked circle. The stake is struck firmly with a mallet, several times if necessary, in order to flatten the bottom sufficiently so that the circle appears on the outside surface of the bowl.

The bottoming stake is now placed solidly in the vise, and the bowl inverted over it. Much care must be taken to assure that the bowl is held in place correctly, so that the circular mark is precisely on the head of the bottoming stake.

The bottom is now finished off by striking slightly outside the stake edge with blows from a sharp wedge-shaped mallet. This "crimps" the metal ever so slightly, to even and flatten the edge of the bottom circle.

The piece is now ready for its final cleaning and polishing.

It is cleaned in the pickling solution, and any fire scale removed with steel wool. Scratches may be removed by buffing with emery cloth. Start with the coarsest grade of emery cloth, then move to the medium grade, and finally to the fine grade. Depending on the degree of polish you desire, you may declare the bowl finished at this point—or go on to the application of Tripoli or rouge polishes, for a mirror finish.

As a final cleaning-up operation, you will file the edges of the bowl smooth. You may have to trim off small projections with shears or a jeweler's saw. A final polish of the edges with emery cloth, and you are ready for enameling.

Since you have spent so much time and so much energy on this piece, it might seem a shame to cover it with opaque enamel. All those laborious hammer blows would be covered. Why not, then, use a clear flux, which will heighten the shine of the metal and protect it from discoloration. An even lovelier effect might be obtained by using transparent enamels—one shade inside the bowl, a contrasting shade on the outside. This is a sort of have-your-cake-and-eat-it solution. You have a lovely spot of color, but all those hammer blows remain for the world to see.

One of the problems in firing any curved shape is warping. After the piece is removed from the kiln, as it cools, the enamel contracts. Since the stresses built up by this contracting enamel tend to vary between the outside and the inside curves, the copper can be pulled out of shape. This need not happen if counteracting measures are taken.

It is really quite simple. The newly fired piece is placed upside down on a clean surface, only a few seconds after it is removed from the kiln. Then a heavy weight is placed on it. Classically, that weight was a flatiron. But these are hardly common objects in households today, and the electric iron simply isn't heavy enough. A brick does nicely, but wrap it in newspaper or paper toweling to avoid any scratching of the copper or enamel surface.

If it is a bowl you have just completed, place it upside down, resting on its rim, on a clean, smooth surface. The brick, wrapped in paper, is then placed on the exposed base of the bowl. Make sure it rests there firmly and squarely. Let it remain until the bowl has cooled completely. For a small bowl, one brick should be sufficient weight. The larger the bowl is, however, the more weight you will need—in which case you simply pile another brick or two atop the first.

CHAPTER 16
MURALS

Creation of a mural presents an irresistible challenge to many a craftsman in enamels. For the most part, enameling is confined to small pieces, limited in size by the kiln in use. After a while this becomes a major frustration. The creative spirit yearns to do something big, something really spectacular.

A mural could be the answer.

The mural, made up of many parts, need have no limitation save that of the space it is to occupy. The design, broken down into small units of proper size to fit into the kiln, are fired one at a time, then assembled like a giant jigsaw puzzle.

Here again, however, the advance planning makes all the difference.

Measure carefully the area you wish filled by the mural. Make a number of sketches until you reach a rough sketch that pleases you and can serve as a take-off point for your final design. Perhaps you are covering the bare wall of a roofed patio with a wild jungle tangle of foliage and flowers, reminiscent of Rousseau. Perhaps you want a floor-to-ceiling panel in your entry hallway "introducing" family members to guests, via hobby and sports symbols. Perhaps you want to cover a problem spot over the kitchen stove with a mural of calorie-laden cakes and sundaes and banana splits.

Decide first how your design can be rendered most effectively. Should it be cut into evenly shaped rectangular sections and later assembled much as one would put up a ceramic-tile wall? Or could it be cut into random rectangular shapes—big squares and little squares and rectangles of various sizes? Perhaps it can be cut up adroitly, jigsaw-puzzle fashion, so that the design itself will camouflage the seams, and the whole will appear to be one huge sheet. Whatever route you take, the design must be broken down into units small enough to fit into your kiln.

Once the design has been decided upon, make a final cartoon of the sketch on a piece of heavy brown wrapping paper, cut precisely to the size of the finished mural. Make your lines bold and strong—a felt-tip pen would be good for this—for they must be traced later.

Assemble the copper you will be using for the project. This can be in large sheets, which you will cut into the smaller-sized units, or you can use odds and ends of scrap copper—if you're lucky enough to find a bargain in these. Just make sure it's all the same thickness.

When the cartoon on the heavy brown paper is finished to your satisfaction, rule it off into squares of the desired dimension. With a colored pen, number these squares, left to right, top to bottom. Then, using artist's tracing paper, use one sheet to trace off that portion of the design that fills each square. If your finished mural has nine units, you will have nine tracing-paper transfers.

The copper tiles you have cut to the dimensions decided upon should be painted with white tempera paint—or any water-soluble white paint, and allowed to dry. Ideally, you would use graphite paper to transfer the design—but this is hard to come by. An acceptable substitute can be created by rubbing the reverse side of your tracing paper sheets with soft pencil. Then the tracing-paper squares are positioned carefully over the painted-copper squares, and the design transferred to the painted copper, using a stylus, or even a ballpoint pen. Be especially careful to follow the lines exactly as they hit the edges of each tile. This is where the design lines up with the adjacent block, and any "off-register" lines will destroy the effectiveness of the whole.

When you have the design transferred to the painted surface, go over the lines again and again, very carefully, with a scribe. Incise the lines of the design into the copper itself. This done, you will wash off the white paint, and clean the copper tile as you would any other copper piece before enameling. But the incised lines will remain to guide you in the enameling process.

With flat tiles, it is particularly important to counterenamel. The reverse side will not be seen, of course, but the counterenamel will help to avert any warping, so that the finished mural can be smooth and flat.

Proceed with the counterenameling and the enameling as you would for any smaller project. Use whatever method of application that seems to fit your design or your style. It might be a good idea to complete the tiles in sequence, lining up each about-to-be-fired tile with its neighbor just completed. In this way you can double-check to make sure the lines flow freely from one tile to the next, and it will be possible to make last-minute adjustments of a fraction of an inch, if necessary.

When all the tiles have been fired, and their edges cleaned and filed, comes the time for assembly. Of course the mural can be cemented directly to the patio wall—but what if you should move? Are you prepared to leave your priceless art work behind? It might be a better idea to assemble the mural on a large sheet of Masonite or Formica, or some other similarly tough but lightweight material. This way, it is not permanently installed, and may be moved if whim dictates at some future date. The tiles may be secured to the backing with a good epoxy glue, or with one of the patented metal-to-wood glues if it is weatherproof.

For dressing up a patio or outdoor entrance foyer, or for any room in the house, it is hard to top the dramatic effect of a well-executed copper-enamel mural. Just be sure it's located in a good light, so all those vibrant colors can really go to work for you.

CHAPTER 17
USING
GLASS GEMS

One of the delightful aspects of copper enameling is the opportunity it presents to go off on wild, wonderful tangents, experimenting with various techniques.

Your kiln heats to a temperature of approximately 1500 degrees—which melts glass. Your powdered enamels are glass, so are the lumps and threads you've used in various designs; therefore, you wonder, why not incorporate other types of glass into your designs?

Craftsmen have been thinking along these lines for years, and have been coming up with some exciting departures from the standard, classic, almost cliché applications of the craft. Cathedral glass, Venetian-glass tiles, glass rods, even bottle glass and shattered glass marbles have been used with amazing effectiveness. Fiber-glass fabrics also have been incorporated into designs which defy description.

But here is a technique where there are no set procedures, no established rules to follow. You must experiment, run samples, try out different temperatures and different timings, before you attempt any finished, polished piece. The chemical composition of different glasses varies so widely—and your kiln is so uniquely itself—that only through this experimentation will you learn how best to get the results you seek.

Glass bits for use on enamel projects may be formed in several ways. The favorite method seems to be to first reduce the glass to chunks of a size which will fit into your kiln. Do this by putting the bottle, or whatever, into a sturdy paper sack and whacking it firmly several times with a mallet or hammer. Each of these pieces is then heated to the dull-red stage, then removed at once from the kiln with tongs and dropped into a pail of cold water. The glass will explode into small bits, along its own natural fracture lines. Most craftsmen agree that this method is preferable to simply pulverizing the glass with repeated hammer blows.

The water is poured out through a sieve, and the retrieved glass fragments spread on paper toweling to dry, then stored in screw-top containers. Be careful to wipe out the pail with paper toweling—small glass splinters may cling to the sides of the pail and be a safety hazard later.

When dry, these fragments may be melted into "jewels" for later use. It is wise to run a series of test firings here, using three different time periods or more. Note the results of each firing, so that you may know precisely how long to fire the bits for the desired results in later projects. The notes on firing times may be stored in the same jar with the glass bits—it could save you time and confusion if you use the bits months later.

Application of the glass "jewels" to an enameled piece may be accomplished in either of two ways. The "jewel" may be positioned directly on the powdered enamel before the first firing, so that it sinks into the enamel as that melts and is secured in that first firing. There is a danger here, however, that some bare metal may show up beneath the "jewel" itself. If that happens, the "jewel" might not adhere snugly to the piece, and fire scale might form on the raw metal, destroying the effectiveness of the "jewel" itself.

The better method is to apply the base-coat enamel, under-fire that, and then position the glass "jewels," using adhesive to make sure they stay where they're put. The second firing, with the "jewels" in position, would bring the piece to the glassy stage, at which time the "jewel" would sink into the enamel and be firmly positioned.

Since your kiln will melt glass, you'll probably want to experiment also with glass fusing. But that's another whole book, with much different techniques than those used in enameling. We heartily recommend Kay Kinney's *Glass Craft*, Chilton Books, 1952.

It is probably only fair and prudent that we issue a word of warning here. Once you've done a bit of experimenting with incorporating glass fragments into your enamel projects, you'll be hooked! You will look at colored glass with entirely new eyes. An old milk-of-magnesia bottle will suddenly become an object devoutly to be desired. You will haunt rummage sales searching for odd glasses in off colors—simply to smash them for glass fragments. You might even covet something from your neighbor's bric-a-brac shelf, simply because it's a shade of green you've never before seen in glass.

And you are due for a few rude shocks. Glass doesn't always come out of the kiln the same color it was when it went in. We learned that the hard way—not being able to get a prior answer from any of the craftsmen we contacted. We are inordinately fond of desert glass—the old, pre-1900 glass that has turned lavender after years of laying on the sand under blazing desert suns. We spent a scorching morning picking up a cupful of shards near the site of a long-defunct desert mine. There were a dozen shades, ranging from amethyst to deep purple. But in the kiln, later, the glass went back to its original white, and stayed there!

Most glass colors, however, are more stable. And there is a special joy in being able to create something exquisitely lovely from materials someone has tossed on the trash heap.

CHAPTER 18
NOW YOU'RE ON YOUR OWN

So there it is—the whole, wide, exciting, challenging world of enameling! You've done each of the simple projects, demonstrating the various techniques easily mastered by the beginner. We hope you've gone on to adapt these directions to still more projects of your own origination.

And now—the sky's the limit. Or, more correctly—the size of your kiln is all that need limit you in any way. And you will find ways to get around *that*. (Remember the chapter on murals?)

First off, of course, we recommend that you read as much as you can find on this subject. The books we have listed in the bibliography that follows are jam-packed with stimulating ideas and instructions for more advanced enamelists.

Perhaps the most satisfying part of having mastered the basic elements of the craft, which we have described in these pages, is the confidence it gives the craftsman. Confidence to strike out and experiment, to try things *not* in the book.

Maybe you'd like to experiment, for instance, with using copper screening in a project of cloisonné or of plique-a-jour. A panel of plique-a-jour, using screen wire, would be ideal as a color spot and safety warning, cemented onto a sliding-glass door.

If you have a friend who is a sewing nut, for the next gift you give her, buy a length of colorful cotton dress fabric, then duplicate the design on half-a-dozen copper buttons. Or, if the budget will stand it, make the fabric silk and the buttons of silver. That will really be an impressive gift.

Try some fiber-glass fabric on the next bowl or tray you fire. You can get fantastic effects with it.

Haunt the bead shops that seem to be proliferating all over the landscape these days, and drive the saleslady wild by buying two of this and three of that—your sole purpose being to melt those glass beads down into decorative spots on your copper pieces. (Warning—always buy an extra button or two, to test first—just to make sure it behaves the way you want it to in the kiln.) Seed beads, bugle beads, odd-shaped beads—they come in unusual shapes and off-colors.

Try using a small butane torch to spot-fuse these beads to your piece, instead of putting them into the kiln. Sometimes the surface oxidation the flame creates gives a gorgeous luster to whatever you're melting. Of course, sometimes it ruins it, too—but you'll never know until you try.

If you have access to a really big kiln, do a coffee-table top design on a stove-door panel you've picked up at a junk yard (for pennies, probably). After all, these are enameled—the base coat is right there waiting for your embellishments.

Get hold of some sample bath or kitchen tiles, the sort

made of steel with an enameled surface. Here again you have a ready-made base coat, just waiting to be decorated.

Graduate from such three-dimensional shapes as bowls and ashtrays, to small sculptural figures. Cut the shapes out of flat copper, bend to suit, then enamel. You could even combine umpty-ump numbers of such shapes into one huge piece for your garden, for instance. Imagine a gigantic enameled butterfly poised in the center of your favorite flower bed!

Try mobiles. Here again is a large, impressive grouping of small parts. But read up on the construction of mobiles first—there's an art to balancing them properly.

Do you have a favorite decorated tile—perhaps an antique ceramic tile? Make a frame for it of enamel—or even a mat and a frame.

Don't neglect the jewelry field. Experiment with rings done in silver cloisonné or a miniature plique-a-jour mobile for earrings. Try a champlevé breastplate-type necklace. Show off your handiwork!

Follow in the footsteps of the pioneering enamelists who have done work on metals other than copper, silver, and gold. See what you can do with brass. It has been successfully enameled after a craftsman discovered some years ago that enamel would adhere to brass if the fire scale was not removed. Try working with aluminum; another enamelist has had sensational results with it, using special, low-fusing enamels and lower temperatures than one would for ordinary copper enameling.

Whatever direction you go, do try an experiment now and then. Who knows—you might come up with some sensational discoveries yourself!

What you do with the skills you've developed is up to you.

Your kiln is there, waiting to be plugged in. The metal is there, waiting, too. And the enamels are there—in every glorious shade of the rainbow. All of them wait only for you to turn them into something you and your friends can enjoy—a thing of beauty.

CHAPTER 19
HISTORY
OF ENAMELING

Enameling is an art which has been around a while—like about two thousand years. Examples of the enameler's art of Greece in the fifth century, B.C. still exist. And it is more than a little awesome to contemplate the fact that today's examples of enamel art will survive much longer than that. Because of refinements in both materials and methods that have come in relatively recent times, enamel pieces are more indestructible than ever.

The earliest pieces of enamel work—at least, those that have been unearthed to this date—were items of personal adornment for those pleasure-loving Greeks and Romans. There may very well have been larger pieces, but in the centuries of wars and looting and pillage, all these have disappeared. They were undoubtedly melted down by their captors for the precious metals they contained. The possibility that such larger figures existed is suggested by the colossal figure of Zeus in the temple at Olympia. The golden draperies of the figure are decorated with enameled figures and flowers, in white and palest blue. But few such examples survived.

Alexander Fisher, one of Britain's foremost enamelists at the turn of this century, wrote of enameling in the *Encyclopaedia Britannica* more than sixty years ago: "It has ever been one of those exquisite arts which exist only under the sunshine of an opulent luxurious time, or sheltered from the rude winds of a poorer age by the affluence of patrons." This statement merits some sober reflection in view of the current surge of interest in enameling.

Interest in the art seems to have dwindled until somewhere between the sixth and ninth centuries, A.D. At least few examples have been found of work created during that period. But the Celts and the Saxons turned out some wondrous gold and bronze ornaments, beginning about 700 A.D. They were adornments for horse trappings, and shields and other personal ornaments.

A classic example of the workmanship of that period can be seen in the Ardagh chalice, on display at the Dublin Museum. By present-day standards, its technique seems curiously primitive, but no less effective. There is also a shield on display in the British Museum which has puzzled enamelists for generations—how did the craftsmen at such an early date obtain that fine opaque red?

From Ireland, the art of enameling was carried to Byzantium. There it reached heights of popularity it has rarely matched since. But the products of the Byzantine enamelist were notably different from those of other areas and other eras. Their colors were confined to the bright primary opaques. No subtle colorations for them. These were introduced later in French, Italian, and Oriental enamels. The Byzantine enamels also had a matte finish, rather than the high gloss in vogue today.

The Byzantines did make one discovery, however, which went almost unheralded. Their craftsmen must have experimented and found that one wet color could be laid next to another wet color, without the two merging—removing the necessity for a wire cloison to separate the colors. Their discovery must not have created much excitement, however, since it was centuries later that the technique was taken up by other enamelists. It was only within the last century that researchers, making microscopic inspection of the Byzantine enamels, actually discovered how these earlier artisans had dispensed with the wire cloisons.

A favorite pilgrimage of enamelists visiting Europe is to view the altar front at Kosterneuberg, which is decorated with fifty champlevé plates executed by one Nicolas of Verdun. There are many other shrines in the area similarly, though less opulently, decorated with examples of the enamelist's art of that period.

The secrets of the craft were next taken to Limoges, and from that area emerged one of the techniques still bearing its name. The artisans of the early fourteenth century in France and Italy must have been endowed with more curiosity and courage for experiment than their predecessors. It was during this period that such techniques as basse-taille and plique-a-jour emerged. Authorities agree that it was due to these artists that enameling finally matured from a decorative art to a fine art.

By the end of the fifteenth century, enamel had escaped its fences. No longer was it purely cloisonné or plique-a-jour.

Grisaille work was first seen, with tones of light enamel laid on a dark base, layer after painstaking layer, until the whole emerged with cameolike detail. Nardon Penicaud was one of the earliest masters of this technique, and many of his works may be seen to this day in the Cluny Museum. He excelled in portraiture.

Among his followers was one Leonard Limosin, who is said to have started the fad in that day and age for using foil. But a fad is a fad is a fad—in any era—and many of the works produced during that time are something less than masterpieces, with their overindulgence in the use of foil.

Perhaps it was this which helped send enameling into a decline for several centuries. It continued to be produced, of course—but with nothing like the popularity it had enjoyed earlier. The courts of France, Russia, and Austria produced some notable enamelists in this period, but not in great numbers. And the art continued to flourish in the Orient, where enamels had been made since the thirteenth century in China, and the late sixteenth century in Japan.

It was late in the nineteenth century that interest in the art was revived, both in Europe and in the United States. Students of history attribute this to the pre-Raphaelite artists who sought a resurgence of interest in things handcrafted, in the face of the onslaughts of the Machine Age.

The irony of this is that today's interest in the art, increasing as it is steadily, month-by-month and year-by-year, is made possible by that very Machine Age. Machines make the small kilns in quantity so that they may be priced within easy reach of almost everyone. Machines form the copper into sizes and shapes easily handled by the home craftsman. Machines package a wider color range of enamels than even the pre-Raphaelite artists dreamed possible, and machines turn out the tools necessary for the enamelist to do the most exacting of detail work.

Even as the artist, with his exquisitely handcrafted objects, fights the flood of mass-produced nonentities of the Machine Age, that very Machine Age keeps grinding out the very means whereby the artist can continue his fight.

CHAPTER 20
WHAT DID I DO WRONG?

Even the most experienced craftsman commits a goof now and then. Attention is diverted from the work-in-hand, and a vital step is inadvertently omitted. The telephone rings, and a piece burns up in the kiln. So don't feel guilty if it happens to you. It's only par for the course. Salvage the piece if you can, following some of the hints we list below. If it can't be saved, chuck it into the trash barrel, write it off as "tuition," and start all over again.

One of the qualifications for a good craftsman is patience. If you weren't born with patience built in, work on developing it. And keep the list below handy for reference, to see where you went wrong if any of your projects go bad. Perhaps you can reclaim them.

Blackened, burned—firing lasted too long. Clean off as much of the overfired enamel as possible with emery cloth, recoat with adhesive and enamel, and refire.

Surface rough, uneven—firing was too brief. Simply put the piece back in the kiln for a minute or two. Watch it closely until it reaches the glassy stage, then take it out.

Cracks in the enamel during cooling—could be either a too-heavy coat of enamel applied initially, or the lack of counterenamel. (The difference in the rates of expansion and contraction between the metal and the enamel sets up tremendous stresses—thus the cracks. Counterenameling will help to reduce the differences in contraction and expansion rates, and help avoid cracks in the future.)

Black spots appear after firing—enamel was not applied evenly and/or thickly enough. Recoat, and refire.

Tiny holes on the surface of the enamel—those are just what they appear to be, burst bubbles. The enamel was still wet when you put it into the kiln, and the moisture formed bubbles which subsequently burst, leaving tiny pockmarks on the surface. Carefully stone away the edges of all the bubbles, refill the marks with enamel, and refire.

Opaque enamels turn transparent—the firing temperature was too high and/or too long. There is no cure for this one, except possibly proceeding as if you'd intended it to be transparent enamel all along!

Finished color not the shade desired—could be due to either too high a kiln temperature or too low a temperature. Certain colors react most sensitively to variations in kiln temperatures. This is why it is so important to make test strips, and to note carefully both firing time and temperature if you have a thermostatically controlled kiln.

Warping (generally in a dish or tray)—piece was not properly or sufficiently weighted during the cooling. As soon as such a piece has been removed from the kiln, and cooled ever so slightly, it should be placed upside down on a firm support and weighted with small heavy object—a flatiron is the classic tool.

Enamel flakes off in great chips—either the copper you're using is too thin, or the enamel was applied too thickly. It might be that you're using the wrong enamel. If none of these seems to apply, it must have been that the copper was insufficiently cleaned before the enamel was applied.

Enamel has spilled over onto kiln floor—this sort of an accident happens to everyone, sooner or later. No, your kiln is not irretrievably damaged. Simply get some kiln wash, or whiting, from your hobby shop, and paint the affected areas with a good, thick coat, allowing it to dry thoroughly before using the kiln again.

GLOSSARY

Acid Resist—Asphalt varnish or asphaltum, painted on metal to protect areas during etching process

Adhesive—Gum tragacanth, agar, gum arabic; powdered gums which, in solution with water, are used to keep powdered enamels in place during firing

Anneal—Process of heating metals, then cooling rapidly, which affects molecular structure so that these metals may be more easily formed

Asbestos Mitten—Any heavily padded mitten, such an as oven mitt, used to protect the hand while working with an open kiln

Asphaltum—A tar product, also called asphalt varnish, used to protect copper in metal etching process

Basse Taille—Process whereby a three-dimensional design is created on metal by chasing, gouging, hammering, etc.; the surface is then coated with transparent enamels

Burnish—To polish highly, preferably with a hard metal disc and power tool

Champlevé—Process wherein depressions are created in metal, through etching or carving; these dimensions are then filled with enamels and fired

Charge—To fill the brush with enamel, or with adhesive

Cloisonné—The process wherein thin metal wires of silver or copper (cloisons) are fastened to the metal base, and used to enclose areas of color

Counterenamel—Enamel coat fired on the back, or reverse, side of any piece, helping to equalize tension and thereby prevent cracking and warping

Crackle Enamel—Enamels available in liquid form, which develop crackle pattern when fired over flux or base-coat enamel on a rounded object but will not crackle on small, flat objects

Dusting—Process of applying enamels through sieve

Element—Heating unit used in electric kilns

Emery Cloth—Used for final polishing of brass; comes in assorted grits

Epoxy Cement—Resin-based glue that forms strong bond on nonporous materials

Etching—Process of removing portions of the surface of metal in an acid solution

Findings—Ready-made parts for jewelry, such as clips and screws for earrings, pinbacks for brooches, etc.

Fire Scale—Black coating that forms on exposed metal while it is in the kiln, the result of oxidation of surface

Flux—In enamels, the colorless transparent enamel; in solder, the ingredient that allows solder to flow

Foil—In enameling, foil is tissue-thin, much thinner than the commonly used household foil

Frit—Chunks of enamel, before they have been reduced to powdered state

Gauge—Measuring until used for metals and wires

Gum Tragacanth—Adhesive used in enameling process

Hard Enamels—Any enamel which fuses at a high temperature, and is not affected by acid

Jewels—Small pieces of fractured glass, melted to a rounded state in the kiln, and then used as decorative spots on enamel

Kiln—An oven firing to high temperatures for enamel work, glass craft, or ceramics; generally electric, but sometimes gas fired

Malleable—Easily bent, or easily cut; not stiff and hard

Mesh—Fineness or coarseness of screen used to sift powdered enamel; i.e., 80-mesh screen has eighty openings per square inch

Mica—Nonmelting mineral material, to which enamels do not adhere

Nichrome—Metal nickel-base alloy that contains chromium and iron, which does not form fire scale in kiln

Nitric Acid—Corrosive acid used in solution for etching metal, and for cleaning copper

Opaque Enamels—Any enamel that covers the metal completely, so that it cannot be seen

Orange-Peel Stage—Enamel that has been incompletely melted due to underfiring, so that its surface texture resembles that of an orange peel

Planishing—The process of toughening and polishing by hammering lightly

Scale Inhibitor—Commercial product painted on surface to protect metal, during firing, from formation of fire scale

Scriber—Sharply pointed metal tool with which designs may be scratched onto metal, or on enameled surfaces

Scrolling—Process of creating designs by stirring molten enamel with special tools while still in the kiln

Sgraffito—Process of obtaining a design by scratching away unfired enamel to reveal fired enamel, or metal, beneath

Sifting—Application of powdered enamels through a fine screen onto the surface being decorated

Soft Enamels—Any enamel that fuses at a low kiln temperature, and is easily affected by acids

Star Stilts—Small starlike constructions of ceramic, with prongs bearing steel tips; used to support enamel pieces in kiln

Stoning—Grinding surface of enamel smooth with carborundum stone, generally done under water

Translucent—Allows light to pass through, but cannot be seen through

Transparent Enamels—Enamel that allows the metal to remain visible through the coats of color

Trivet—Support to hold enamel piece during firing

Warping—Bending metal out of shape

BIBLIOGRAPHY

Some of the books listed here are still in print and may be obtained at your local bookshop or at a craft and hobby shop. Others, though out of print, can be found sometimes in used book stores. If there is a particular title you want but cannot locate at the sources available to you, you might want to try one of the book-search services, such as Books-on-File, Box 195, Union City, New Jersey, 07087, or one of the services listed in the "Out-of-Print" classification in the advertisements in the *Saturday Review.*

Amaco. *Metal Enameling Handbook.* Indianapolis: American Art Clay Co., 1971.

Bates, Kenneth F. *Enameling Principles and Practice.* Cleveland: World Publishing, 1951.

Bates, Kenneth F. *The Enamelist.* Cleveland: World Publishing, 1967.

Clarke, Geoffrey, and Frances Feher. *The Technique of Enameling.* New York: Reinhold, 1967.

Dutton, Ninette. *The Beautiful Art of Enamelling.* London: ARC Books, 1966 (now available in paperback).

"Enamels." *Encyclopaedia Britannica.*

Gick, James, *Copper Enameling.* Inglewood, Calif.: Arts and Crafts Publishers, 1957.

Maryon, Herbert. *Metalworking and Enameling.* New York: Watson-Guptill Publications, 1958 (now available in paperback).

Newble, Brian. *Practical Enamelling and Jewelry Work.* New York: Viking Press, 1967.

Pack, Greta. *Jewelry and Enameling.* New York: D. Van Nostrand, 1941.

Pack, Greta. *Jewelry and Enameling.* New York: D. Van Nostrand, 1941.

Rebert, Jo, and O'Hara, Jean. *Copper Enameling.* Columbus, Ohio: Professional Publications, 1956.

Rothenberg, Polly. *Metal Enameling.* New York: Crown Publishers, 1969.

Search Books. *Homemade Enamel Jewelry.* London: Search Books, 1967.

Seeler, Margaret. *The Art of Enameling.* New York: Van Nostrand Reinhold, 1969.

Thompson, Thomas E. *Enameling on Copper and Other Metals.* Highland Park, Ill.: T. C. Thompson, 1950.

Untracht, Oppi. *Enameling on Metal.* Philadelphia and New York: Chilton Co., 1957.

Winter, Edward. *Enamel Art on Metals.* New York: Watson-Guptill Publications, 1958.

Zechlin, Katharina. *Creative Enamelling and Jewelry Making.* New York: Sterling Publishing Co., 1965.

SUPPLIERS

Many of the suppliers listed below offer catalogs and/or brochures describing their merchandise. Some charge a nominal fee for these catalogs, some do not. We suggest a postcard inquiry preceding any request for a catalog.

American Art Clay Co., Inc.
4717 West Sixteenth Street
Indianapolis, Indiana 46222
Kilns; enameling, ceramic
   supplies

American Handicrafts
1900 Windsor Place
Fort Worth, Texas 76110
*Kilns; enameling, handi-
    craft supplies*
*Write here for catalog and
    information regarding
    the store nearest you.*

Allcraft Tool & Supply Co.,
    Inc.
215 Park Avenue
Hicksville, New York 11801
Kilns; enameling supplies

AKG & Company
1114 Greentree Road
Newark, Delaware 19711
*Kilns; enameling, handi-
    craft supplies*

Bergen Arts & Crafts
P.O. Box 689
Salem, Massachusetts 01970
*Kilns; enameling, handi-
    craft supplies*

Dick Blick
P.O. Box 1267
Galesburg, Illinois 61401
*Kilns; enameling, handi-
    craft, art supplies*

Craft Carnival
13629 Victory Boulevard
Van Nuys, California 91401
Kilns; enameling supplies

Gager's Handicraft
3516 Beltline Boulevard
St. Louis Park, Minnesota
   55416
*Kilns; enameling, handi-
   craft supplies*

Grieger's, Inc.
1633 East Walnut Street
Pasadena, California 91109
Jewelry findings

T.B. Hagstoz & Son
709 Sansom Street
Philadelphia, Pennsylvania
   19106
*Jewelry metal, supplies,
   tools*

C.R. Hill Co.
35 W. Grand River Avenue
Detroit, Michigan 48226
*Kilns; enameling, jewelry
   supplies*

Immerman's Crafts, Inc.
21668 Libby Road
Cleveland, Ohio 44137
*Kilns; enameling, jewelry
   supplies*

Kraft Korner
5842 Mayfield Road
Mayland Annex
Cleveland, Ohio 44124
Kilns; enameling, handi-
craft supplies

Kit Kraft
12109 Ventura Place
Studio City, California
91602
Kilns; enameling, handi-
craft supplies

Leisure Crafts
P.O. Box 5528
Compton, California 90221
Kilns; enameling, handi-
craft supplies

L and L Manufacturing Co.
142 Conchester Road
Twin Oaks, Pennsylvania
19016
Kilns

Paragon Industries, Inc.
P.O. Box 10133
Dallas, Texas 75207
Kilns

Skil-Crafts
P.O. Box 105
Joplin, Missouri 64801
Kilns; enameling, handi-
craft supplies

Thomas C. Thompson Co.
P.O. Box 127
Highland Park, Illinois
   60035
Kilns; enameling supplies

INDEX